THE PSALMS OF DAVID

The Psalms of David

TRANSLATED FROM THE SEPTUAGINT
GREEK BY DONALD SHEEHAN

Xenia Sheehan and Hierodeacon Herman Majkrzak, EDITORS
Foreword by Christopher Merrill
Preface by the Very Rev. John Breck

WIPF & STOCK · Eugene, Oregon

THE PSALMS OF DAVID
Translated from the Septuagint Greek by Donald Sheehan

Copyright © 2013 Carol Xenia Sheehan. All rights reserved. Except for brief quotations in critical publications or reviews, no part of this book may be reproduced in any manner without prior written permission from the publisher. Write: Permissions, Wipf and Stock Publishers, 199 W. 8th Ave., Suite 3, Eugene, OR 97401.

Wipf & Stock
An Imprint of Wipf and Stock Publishers
199 W. 8th Ave., Suite 3
Eugene, OR 97401
www.wipfandstock.com

ISBN 13: 978-1-62032-5100

Manufactured in the U.S.A.

Portions of this Psalms translation first appeared in Thomas Nelson, *The Orthodox Study Bible: Ancient Christianity Speaks to Today's World* (O.T. © St. Athanasius Academy of Orthodox Theology, 2008; N.T. text © Thomas Nelson, 1982). All material herein that resulted from Donald Sheehan's work in assisting the Academy in writing The Orthodox Study Bible is used by permission of the Academy, which has released any claim on its copyright to Carol Sheehan, her heirs and assigns.

Psalms 102, 132, and 150 were previously published, in a differently lineated version, in the *St. Petersburg Review* 4/5, 2011/12.

Hand-drawn graphics by Andrew Gould, © New World Byzantine Studios, used by permission in this edition.

This translation of the Psalter is dedicated to Carol Xenia,
'Thou whom my soul loves.' (Song of Solomon 1:7)

CONTENTS

Foreword by Christopher Merrill ix
Preface by the Very Rev. John Breck xi
Translator's Preface xv
Acknowledgments xxiii
Introduction: The Mind of David and the Mind of Christ xxv

THE PSALMS OF DAVID 1

Bibliography 173

Appendix on Numbering of Psalms and Praying the Kathismata 175

FOREWORD

O TASTE AND SEE

THE PSALMS ARE FIRST and foremost poems—of praise and prayer, of bewilderment and righteous indignation, of love and loss. They offer prophesies, instruction, solace, thanksgiving, testimony, history, law—in short, the full range of responses to the human condition, in the singular voice of the poet or poets known as David: the Psalmist who distilled the yearnings of the ancient Israelites and made of his walk in the sun one hundred and fifty poems, which form the ground of our spiritual inheritance. They are by turns angry and tender, defiant and beseeching, and they are beautiful. The hymnbook of Jews and Christians, the Psalter has schooled generations in the mystery of worship, the consolations of faith, the agony of doubt; its cadences and images, its style of thought and argument, have long shaped the Western literary imagination; in English, the music of the King James Version of the Psalms can be heard in poets as different as William Blake, Walt Whitman, and Richard Wilbur, not to mention songwriters like Leonard Cohen and Bono, whose credits include an introduction to an edition of the Psalms. "O taste and see," the Psalmist advises. This is what we do whenever we take him at his word.

What a blessing it is to have this English version of the Septuagint Psalter—the Greek translation of the Hebrew Bible, which according to tradition was commissioned by Ptolemy II in the third century B.C., in Alexandria, capital of the Hellenic world. Here is the poetry that was on the tongues of Jesus and his disciples, in teaching and at table, in prayer and on the cross. To read these Psalms, then, silently or aloud, in solitude or in congregation, is to enact a return to the origins of Christianity. For it was in the praying of the Psalms that early Christians gave voice to their hopes and fears in the aftermath of the Passion, obeying in these communal promptings of the spirit the commands of the resurrected Christ. Verset by verset, they recalled their obligations here below, prayed for the life to come, celebrated the healing power of faith; they discovered shapes for the idea of the divine vouchsafed to them

ix

Foreword

by the Lord, the new covenant, and created a tradition of worship, which continues to sustain the Church—a tradition rooted in the poetry of the Psalms, which Donald Sheehan has expertly captured in this magnificent translation.

Indeed his version of the Psalms is at once faithful to the original text, richly musical, and marked by the sorts of ingenious solutions perhaps discoverable only in a life governed by poetry and prayer. A professor, poet, and the longtime director of the Frost Place, Sheehan devoted his final years to rendering into English the Psalms, which he had prayed daily for over two decades. Which is to say: their shaping influence on his spiritual life took poetic form as he plumbed their depths, seeking their multiple meanings, tinkering with one word and then another, comparing the Hebrew text to the Greek, listening for echoes from his wide reading and experience. That he did not settle for the first word that came to mind, or the fifth, is apparent in every Psalm, which he treats as a whole unto itself. And his determination to preserve the poetry is what will ensure that this Psalter stands the test of time—that readers take it to heart.

The Polish poet Zbigniew Herbert likens the translator of poetry to a bumblebee alighting on a flower, unable to taste anything (he has a cold) as he elbows his way to the yellow pistil, avid for sweetness, and then swaggers on to the next flower, his nose sticky with pollen. It is an endearing image of a much-scorned literary figure (without whom our interior lives would be much impoverished), which is as far removed from the practice of Donald Sheehan as can be imagined. His Psalter works as poetry, because it was born of humility and brought to perfection by dint of hard work and the grace of God. Call it providential—a marriage of translator and text, which reads as if it was made in Heaven. O *taste and see.*

Christopher Merrill
Director, International Writing Program, University of Iowa

PREFACE

TRANSLATION IS AN ART that involves a certain ascetic discipline. It requires one to enter so fully into the language to be rendered into another tongue that the original language and its meaning become one's own.

A good translation does not simply render a text word for word, nor does it consist of a paraphrase that reproduces only an approximation of the original meaning. This is especially true with translations of sacred texts. To produce a "good" translation of the Holy Scriptures—one that conveys beauty as well as sense—the translator needs to approach the text globally, holistically, in order to penetrate to the depths of its intended message. That message, however, is only partially expressed by words, sentences, and all the components that make up a literary unit. While remaining faithful to the generally accepted meaning of words, the translator will find meaning beyond the words themselves through a process of "communion." One takes the text into oneself, as it were, in order to grasp its ultimate meaning at the level of the heart as well as of the mind. Truly to understand the text, and thus to be able to render it into another language, the translator needs to hear and even "feel" its meaning. In the case of Scripture, this implies that one move beyond a rational understanding of the message conveyed by a given passage, to embrace and be embraced by the Subject of that message.

In recent years a great deal of attention has been given to what is termed "reader-response criticism." This approach, with rhetorical criticism in general, grew out of the perception that a text is dynamic. Its meaning is not fixed, but varies according to the perspective of the reader. This is the phenomenon that leads to widely divergent interpretations of passages of the Bible. Post-Enlightenment forms of exegesis have focused mainly on the "literal sense" of a text: the meaning the biblical author sought to convey by his writings. Since the earliest centuries of Christian biblical interpretation, exegetes have nevertheless recognized that a text conveys more than a literal meaning. Consequently, they have often employed allegory and typology as interpretive tools, to enable them to discern behind and beyond the "intention of the author" a deeper, fuller, or more complete meaning, a *sensus plenior*, that could

Preface

be applied to the reader's moral and spiritual life (in medieval Latin exegesis, the "tropological" and "anagogical" senses of Scripture). Reader-response criticism builds on these intuitions by acknowledging that there exists a dynamic relationship between the text and the reader (termed respectively the "artistic" and the "aesthetic" poles), such that the reader can constantly derive new understanding or a fresh message from a frequently read and well-known passage. To secular literary critics, this occurs as a function of the changing circumstances in the reader's life that lead that reader to approach the text with ever differing perspectives. The "dynamic" occurs between the written word and the reader's immediate and contingent perception of its meaning, which can, of course, lead to pure relativism: a text "means" whatever my mental or psychological state may bring to it at any given time. To the Christian interpreter, and translator, this "dynamic"—the capacity of the text to convey new meaning in different situations and changing circumstances—is a function of the inspirational activity of the Holy Spirit.

In rendering the Greek "Septuagint" version of the biblical Psalms into fresh and yet traditional English, Donald Sheehan has produced a translation that conveys the "literal" sense of the text with power and beauty. Yet his sensitivity to the symbolic value of language has enabled him to use words in such a way as to move the reader beyond an intellectual grasp of the psalmist's message to a level of understanding that represents a true *sensus plenior*. This is "translation" in the pure sense of the term. It represents the "intention of the biblical author," the original meaning of a psalm as it was initially composed, in its specific historical, sociological, and spiritual setting. At the same time, this translation—thoroughly faithful to that literal sense—conveys to the reader a new depth of perception through which the text itself can reveal a deeper, fuller meaning that speaks to the reader's own immediate circumstances.

In this rendering, the Psalms become once again what they were for Christian believers from the very beginning: the hymnal of the Church. They remain, certainly, the songs of Israel: from its cries of lamentation to its shouts of exultation. But for the Christian reader, they become as well hymns of petition and praise that express both the joy and the longing of those who live "in Christ."

They do so, because the translator has "entered into" the original Greek with sensitivity and appreciation, to offer us a Psalter of rare beauty and power. Thereby he offers the reader the possibility not only to hear the psalmist's own voice, but to make of these hymns a means of communication—of genuine communion—between the reader and the God of whom the Psalms speak and to whom they make their appeal. The Psalms can become, then, our prayer addressed to the God of Israel and the Church. And at the same time their very language can convey to us the assurance that, as he has throughout the millennia, God hears that prayer and responds to it with boundless mercy, love, and compassion.

As the child's voice spoke to St. Augustine: "Take up and read!" Take up this fine translation of the Psalter and allow the language itself to convey to both your mind and your heart the truth and the beauty of its timeless and life-giving message.

Archpriest John Breck
Professor Emeritus, Saint Sergius
Theological Institute, Paris

TRANSLATOR'S PREFACE

TRADITION HAS IT THAT seventy-two scholars, six from each of the twelve tribes of Israel, were assembled in Alexandria sometime in the second or third century B.C. to translate the Hebrew Scriptures into Greek. Hebrew was understood by relatively few people at that time, mostly scholars, while Greek was the *lingua franca* of the Roman empire. They worked for forty days, one legend goes, in separate tents, producing in the end a translation that agreed in every word. It is called the translation of the Seventy, or the Septuagint, abbreviated as LXX.

With the destruction of Jerusalem in 70 A.D., most Hebrew texts were lost, and it wasn't until much later (between the seventh and tenth centuries) that the Masoretes assembled what had survived and, drawing on oral tradition, refashioned a Hebrew Bible or Tanakh. It is on this Masoretic text that most Bibles in English are based. But the Greek Septuagint, used continuously in Eastern Orthodox Christian worship and the source of Old Testament quotations in the New Testament, reflects a considerably older and unbroken Hebrew tradition. My Hebrew teacher, visiting Dartmouth College from Hebrew University in Jerusalem, once told me that, "Of course we correct the Hebrew from the Greek."

Working from the 1979 edition of Alfred Rahlfs' Septuagint Psalter, my primary aim in making this translation was to create in English a body of poetry that, in employing the rich idioms of contemporary English poetics, would stand on its own in cadence and shape. My many years as a university teacher of both ancient and modern lyric poetry, along with my work of reading, writing, and translating poetry—both privately and professionally—guided me to see that each psalm possessed a unique *cadential shape* in every line as well as in each whole poem.

I soon discovered something of what Mother Maria had found in translating the Hebrew Psalter:[1] that every psalm has a unique face; that is, each psalm possesses something very like personhood. I found the lexical meanings of the Greek words would therefore illumine the musical shape of my

---

1 *The Psalms: An Exploratory Translation.*

xv

Translator's Preface

translation just as the English cadences would help reveal to me more fully the Greek meanings.

I also consulted the Hebrew text in working on the Greek, thereby gaining a growing awareness of and insight into the remarkable achievement of the LXX translators. In the penultimate chapter of Second Samuel, for example, we are given the final words of David as he is dying. His last words are a tiny psalm, the first line of which is: "The spirit of the Lord has spoken by me, and His word was on my tongue" (2 Sam 23:2).[2] The Hebrew for this line is (as biblical Hebrew always is) extremely beautiful. Transliterated, the line looks and sounds approximately like this:

Ru-áh Adonai diber-bi umilatho al-l'shoni.

These five words (actually, word-clusters) themselves form a tiny chiastic pattern,[3] with the verb *diber-bi* ("he has spoken") providing the center:

Ru-áh
    Adonai
        diber-bi
    umilatho
al-l'shoni

The spirit of God (*ru-áh Adonai*) powerfully descends into the center of His having spoken. Then out from the center there arises the comparably strong incarnation of God's word on David's tongue. Now, the rhythmic movement of the Hebrew line is slow, and dense, and inexorable, like tidal movements onto an ocean beach. Syllabic echoes serve to punctuate this rhythm: the *-bi* at the center is rhymed with the *-ni* at the end; the vowel sound in the *-áh* that ends the first word is echoed in the *al-* that begins the last word. Such echoings help to sculpt the rhythm into its densely comprehensible shape. The final effect is indeed oceanic: the wave's long, slow surge onto the beach followed by its comparably powerful and deliberate withdrawal back into the ocean. This is the characteristic rhythm of much biblical Hebrew poetry.

  2 See p. xxv, n. 2 below, regarding the author's English renderings of Scripture. —Ed.

  3 In this pattern, the first and the final lines of a given biblical passage connect to one another; then the second line connects to the next-to-last line; the third line connects to the third-to-last; and so on, until an exact midpoint is reached. See Breck, *Biblical Language*. See also the introduction, "The Mind of David and the Mind of Christ," herein.

Translator's Preface

When the second-century B.C. Greek translators rendered this line in the Septuagint translation, they did so this way:

Pnévma Kyríou elálisen en eme, ke o lógos avtoú epí glossis mou.

What is most interesting in this Greek is its extreme literalness. So extreme is it, in fact, that it here disarrays ordinary Greek syntax in order to reflect a key feature of Hebrew: that is, the phrase *en eme* is placed *after* the verb so as to catch something of the suffixing so characteristic of Hebrew verbs. Here, and almost everywhere, Septuagint Greek will go to great lengths to sustain the accuracy of its mapping.

But the rhythmic movement of the Greek line could not be more unlike Hebrew. Where the Hebrew moves oceanically, the Greek moves balletically. Thus, rather than being carried on slow, strong tidal movements, we are instead brought into a quick, bright, and intricate dance as it is being perfectly executed. And so assured is the line's rhythmic movement that it can even execute a Hebrew 'gesture' and never lose its perfect balance: such is everywhere the genius of Septuagint Psalmic Greek. In this way, the final effect of the Greek rhythm may best be seen as one of balletic perfection. Thus, while being vastly different, the Greek rhythm is nevertheless an admirable *counter-response* to the Hebrew: a response, that is, that fully matches but never anywhere attempts to rival the Hebrew reality it is responding to.

In this sense, then, Septuagint Greek gives itself in love to the Hebrew original, in an act of *kenosis*.[4] For on every single page, almost in every sentence and phrase, we can witness how the Greek language is *dying to itself* so that the Hebrew may live. It dies the death of its own syntactic coherence, over and over, a coherence fully and beautifully established in Homer and brought to a luminous magnificence in Pindar, Sophocles, and Plato. Yet each time Septuagint Greek willingly dies in love for biblical Hebrew, it enters into that perfective stillness we call eternal memory.[5] And here, in this realm of eternal

4   *Kenosis* is a Greek word meaning "emptiness" or "self-emptying." Its use in Christian theology derives from Philippians 2:5–7: "In your minds you must be the same as Christ Jesus. His state was divine, yet he did not cling to his equality with God but emptied Himself to assume the condition of a slave and became as men are" (Jerusalem Bible translation). Thus it is the self-emptying of one's own will in order to become entirely receptive to the perfect will of God. —Ed.

5   "Eternal memory" is the Orthodox funeral prayer that the life of the righteous departed may be remembered by God, inscribed in the

Translator's Preface

memory, Septuagint Greek achieves its immense significance: it becomes *zoópios*, "life-giving." For here Septuagint Greek remembers and is remembered by the God of Abraham, Isaac, and Jacob at the very same moment it foresees this central fact of the Gospels: that when, two centuries hence, Our Lord will quote Scripture, He will do so, sometimes via an Aramaic version, in Septuagint Greek. Such are the life-giving actions of eternal memory.

In measuring the arc from biblical Hebrew to LXX Greek, I came to understand more clearly the relational work every translation must accomplish. As the Hebrew was being, at every moment, uprooted and replanted by and in the Greek, the living personhood of each psalm deepened and changed in the sense that any plant is changed by being uprooted from the soil where it has grown to fruitfulness. Yet the Hebrew psalm's unique shape was unalterably recognizable in the new Greek soil. It was breathtaking to behold. I would find myself altering a word—very often a syllable—of my English to reflect more fully something of the relational reality existing between LXX Greek and biblical Hebrew.

Hence, my constant hope was that my work on English cadential shape and Greek lexical meaning would help bring my versions closer to the beautiful soil wherein the LXX translators had established that living relationship between their Psalms and the Hebrew originals, thereby giving richer shape and deeper meaning to my English. Such was my deepest hope for these Psalms; such, indeed, was my prayer.

In this translation, I have sought to avoid the pitfalls of taking either side in the contemporary debate about archaic versus modern language. I have sought, that is, to avoid both the impenetrability of the willfully archaic and the breeziness of the merely modern. The Psalms, in both biblical Hebrew and Septuagint Greek, possess astonishing depths of clarity and dignity in word, phrase, line, and whole poem. My guiding intention has been to render them as faithfully as I could, through the medium of the English I know and love.

Book of Life, and so bear fruit in the Kingdom. "Truly, truly I say to you, Unless the seed of wheat fall into the ground and die, it abides alone; but if it die, it brings forth much fruit" (John 12:24). To act *kenotically* in life, following Christ, is to prepare the way for this fruitfulness and even, in some measure, to achieve the promised stillness *in life* through *theosis*, god-becoming (see n. 8). —*Ed.*

Translator's Preface

I began this phase of my Psalms translation with the Orthodox Study Bible project, which used the New King James text as a base;[6] but I often found myself departing from that text so as more accurately to engage the Greek. I have now departed further, primarily in restoring the distinction, lost in modern English, between the second-person singular and plural pronouns—a distinction strongly and beautifully present in both Greek and Hebrew. I found that I had been missing that peculiarly intimate language of love that moves in our relations with God and with our friends, and even with our enemies (as we are commanded!)—in the singular, one by one. On this point I remember years ago being in the living room of an elderly Quaker couple as the husband asked each of us if we would like some tea and then turned to his wife: "Dost thou want some too?" I heard in this the language of unique love. Even more than conveying intimacy, however, the singular second-person pronoun is a more faithful rendering of the Greek and Hebrew originals. It is significant for Christians that we always address God in the singular, even when we address Him as Trinity. This distinction in number is quite clear in Greek and Hebrew—indeed, it is clear in nearly every language—but it is absent in modern English, where we use the same second-person pronoun for both singular and plural.

The use of *thee, thou, thy,* and *thine* of course required the appropriate verb forms. But this in turn added syllables and changed the cadence and sonic quality of the text in a number of places. To correct for this I have made further verbal changes, mostly in word order and verb mode (though never departing from the meaning of the Greek), where too many of the archaic verb endings would otherwise seem to intrude on the reader or break the cadence. For example, in Psalm 84:5: "Couldst thou really be angry forever? Couldst thou prolong thine anger from generation to generation?" becomes "Couldst thou really be angry forever, prolonging thine anger from generation to generation?"

In the presence of the second-person singular pronouns, it soon became clear that the capitalization of pronouns for God (used primarily to distinguish the divine *You* from all others) was no longer necessary. Without it, we are no worse off than a reader of the Greek in those passages where one must

---

6   Thomas Nelson, *The Orthodox Study Bible: Ancient Christianity Speaks to Today's World* (OT: St. Athanasius Academy of Orthodox Theology, 2008; NT text: Thomas Nelson, 1982). All material herein that resulted from Donald Sheehan's work in assisting the Academy in writing *The Orthodox Study Bible* is used by permission of the Academy. —Ed.

Translator's Preface

puzzle out who is speaking or being spoken to (as in the intimate dialogue between the psalmist and God in Psalm 90), or who is acting (as in the web of shifting pronoun referents in Psalm 104). I went on to adopt (with a few exceptions) the practice of the 1611 King James translators, capitalizing (besides place names, names of persons, and the first words of quotations) only those words used as names for God such as *Lord* and *Holy One, Most High, King, Holy Spirit,* and *Christ* (which I have used because it best translates the Greek *christos* and looks forward to the Lord's incarnation, always prefigured in His great ones).

In the Eastern Orthodox Church, to which I belong, the Psalms are central to liturgical life and are most often chanted, in both parish churches and monasteries. One practice in both personal and monastic prayer is to chant through the entire Psalter each week, assigning certain *kathismata* (literally, "sittings") to each day. At least by the twelfth century, a division of the Psalter into twenty *kathismata* had been established for this purpose. I have indicated these divisions, and their subdivisions into *stases*, in my text. I have also, of course, followed the Septuagint numbering of the psalms and Rahlfs' numbering of verses. The reader will find at the end of the book a table of Greek vs. Hebrew psalm numbering, as well as a list of the *kathismata* to be prayed each day of the week.

Four further notes about this translation: Although I have adopted a more traditional (in English) lineation of the Psalms in this edition,[7] I have followed the Greek in Psalm 118 by using a two-line mini-stanza. I do so because I am seeking to create something like the Greek's balletic movements between call and response, and counter-call and counter-response, between the "I" of the psalmic speaker and the "Thou" of the divine presence—in ways that recall something of the Hebrew alphabetic repetitions. Thus, the effect I am after is this: the "I" defers to the "Thou" only to have the "Thou" then bow gracefully to the "I" in a way that prompts the "I" to further response. In so moving this way, the "I" can be seen as entering into direct participation in the movements of "Thou," while the "Thou" can be seen as moving toward the "I." In this way, the divine Thou moves toward *kenosis* (self-emptying) while the human moves toward *theosis* (deification).[8]

---

7 In some earlier versions Dr. Sheehan had used short lines, two to four for each verse. —Ed.

8 See n. 4 on *kenosis*. *Theosis* or deification "literally means to become gods by Grace. The Biblical words that are synonymous and descriptive of Theosis are: adoption, redemption, inheritance, glorification, holiness and perfection. Theosis is the acquisition of the Holy Spirit,

Translator's Preface

I have included the Masoretic Hebrew word *selah* at certain points in the text, rather than the Septuagint word *diapsalma*. Both words are of unknown meaning and therefore untranslatable, but I felt it better to use the more familiar Hebrew word than the completely unknown Greek one. Gregory of Nyssa says in his *Treatise on the Inscriptions of the Psalms*:

> We have understood some such meaning of *diapsalma* as follows. If some illumination of the Holy Spirit in regard to other matters occurred in the midst of David's prophesying, as the singing of the psalm was proceeding consistently, and some additional grace of knowledge for the benefit of those receiving the prophecy, he held his speech in check for a moment and let his understanding receive the knowledge of the thoughts which occurred to him from the divine illumination.[9]

I have also included the Septuagint inscriptions (or "titles") at the beginning of each psalm, though I have not followed the more common Greek practice of numbering them as line 1.

A final note on punctuation: I have tried to be as light as possible, using the least amount of punctuation necessary for meaning and flow. Psalms are meant to be chanted, to move quickly and with sober grace. I hope that these will do so.

The lexicons used in this translation are: *The New Brown-Driver-Briggs-Gesenius Hebrew and English Lexicon* (1979); Hatch and Redpath, *Concordance to the Septuagint* (1998); Lampe, *A Patristic Greek Lexicon* (1961); Liddell, Scott, Jones, *Greek-English Lexicon* (1968); Lust, Eynikel, Hauspie, Chamberlain, *A Greek-English Lexicon of the Septuagint*, Part I (1992) and Part II (1996); and Taylor, *The Analytical Lexicon to the Septuagint* (1994). Besides Alfred Rahlfs' *Septuaginta* (1979), other texts consulted include Brenton, *The Septuagint Version, Greek and English* (1970); and *The Interlineary Hebrew and English Psalter* (1979).

Donald Sheehan

---

whereby through Grace one becomes a participant in the *Kingdom of God*. Theosis is an act of the uncreated and infinite love of God. It begins here in time and space, but it is not static or complete, and is an open-ended progression uninterrupted through all eternity." Archimandrite George, *Theosis*, 86.—Ed.

9 Heine, *Treatise*, 157–58.

ACKNOWLEDGMENTS

THIS VOLUME REPRESENTS A long labor of love on the part of many people. If Don were alive, he would wish to thank them personally, by name—his Hebrew teacher at Dartmouth College, for instance; those teachers and scholars who helped him in his study of Greek; Dartmouth College for a typing grant; Maria Hillhouse for an enormous labor of typing and formatting that cost her the motherboard of her computer; forgive me, I have surely forgotten others.

From the very beginning, going back well into the last century, when Don's translation of Psalms first focused on "correcting" his King James Psalter to reflect the Greek Septuagint for his own prayer, friends too numerous to mention have wanted copies for their prayer. It is really these friends who have kept the project going; and when, a few years ago, we sought financial help to self-publish this final translation, our friends were generously supportive. Don's repose intervened and the project stalled, but it is the funds they contributed then that have made the current publication possible.

In 2001, Don was asked to participate in the Old Testament Orthodox Study Bible project undertaken by St. Athanasius Academy of Orthodox Theology with the blessing of Metropolitan Philip and the help of Thomas Nelson, publisher of the *New King James Bible* and *The Orthodox Study Bible* (New Testament). The goal of this project was to conform the New King James Old Testament text to the ancient Greek Septuagint (LXX), with carefully written study notes. He took on a third of the Psalter, then another third, and then the entire Book of Psalms, carving hundreds of hours out of his already full life to do this. I wish to acknowledge and give thanks, on Donald Sheehan's behalf, to St. Athanasius Academy and The Orthodox Study Bible committee for giving him the opportunity and salutary deadlines to accomplish the work, and for bringing the Old Testament Septuagint into readable English. I wish also to thank the many people from several western parishes who took the time to decipher and type his handwritten copy. And I thank Paul Goetz, Administrator of St. Athanasius Academy, for giving his blessing

Acknowledgments

to the publication of the present volume, in which much of the material is substantially the same as that published in *The Orthodox Study Bible* (Old Testament) Book of Psalms, although much is different.

On Don's behalf, I wish here to thank our sons, David and Rowan Benedict, for their gracious acceptance of their father's sacrifice of his time and health to this work of Psalms translation and study, which did not end with the Study Bible project.

I thank Sydney Lea for his long and faithful friendship to Don, for offering his support to my project of posthumously publishing Don's work, and for encouraging me to try Wipf and Stock, a good publisher.

I am indebted to Matthew Baker and to John Taylor Carr for their wisdom and generosity in helping me to clarify some theological matters in the introduction. I know Don would have been grateful for this as well.

I want to thank Don's godson Hierodeacon Herman (Majkrzak) for his careful advice and critique at many crucial points, for his countless hours of typing and formatting the Psalter for what was to be a self-published leather-bound prayer book, and, finally, for his editorial and typographical design work on the present volume. And I thank Andrew Gould of New World Byzantine Studios for his willingness to facilitate the self-published prayer edition (which, God willing, may yet see the light of day at some future time) and for his brilliant illuminations, which grace this edition.

Don, as I stand at the beginning of a path that I hope leads into Orthodox monastic life, my prayer is that this publication of your beautiful Psalms, filled with your love for David and for God—which has inspired and deepened my own—will add to your store of treasure in the Heavenly Kingdom. And I hope that I may now at last follow your example in psalmic prayer. You did this when you had no free time; it seems I must change my whole life to do it.

Xenia Sheehan

INTRODUCTION
The Mind of David and the Mind of Christ

I.

MY EXPERIENCE IN PRAYING the Psalms for over two decades has given me a tiny, fleeting glimpse of a vast and very great subject. I can put the subject this way: the Psalms disclose the mind of David in the process of becoming the mind of Christ.[1] The fundamental question, therefore, is, How do the Psalms accomplish this?

The phrase "the mind of Christ" is of course St. Paul's, when, in First Corinthians, he writes this astonishing sentence: "We have the mind of Christ" (2:16).[2] St. Paul's point in this chapter of the epistle is that we possess in ourselves the mind of Christ *solely because* God has given us this mind in order that we may know—in St. Paul's own words—"the things freely given us by God" (1 Cor 2:12). Itself a gift, the mind of Christ in us is thus the mode wherein we know God's gifts. For St. Paul, then, the essence of our mental life can best be expressed as human gratitude for divine self-giving.

---

1 Fr. John Breck has written, "In this perspective, the Church's attribution of the Psalms (en bloc) to David ... is a matter of ecclesial affirmation of a particular tradition (the Jews also recognized that the psalms were from various authors at various periods in the people's history, yet they honored and honor them as 'Davidic'). It confirms the legitimate *authority* of the writings in question ... [A]ll of us begin 'with the mind of David' with the hope and intention of moving toward 'the mind of Christ.'" E-mail to the editor, 14 June 2012. —*Ed.*

2 Scripture quotations in this essay are the author's own translations from the Septuagint Greek, generally Rahlfs' *Septuaginta*. They are occasionally slightly paraphrased or adapted to context, but always annotated. The published version closest to his phrasings is often the English Standard, though the English he long used in his own prayer was the King James, "corrected" to the Septuagint. References to Psalms use the Septuagint numbering, for which see the appendix. —*Ed.*

Introduction

To help understand the ways wherein St. Paul's immense insight can illumine the Psalms, I shall consider two crucial chapters—the sixteenth and seventeenth—in the Davidic narratives in First Samuel. In these chapters, we can distinguish three moments that, taken together, beautifully reveal what I am calling the mind of David. The first moment occurs when the prophet Samuel comes to the house of Jesse to choose a new king to replace Saul, the first king of Israel. David is the eighth, and youngest, son of Jesse. Now, his status in his father's house is made plain when Jesse brings each of his eldest seven sons to Samuel in order of age, hoping each time that Samuel will choose *this* son as king. But Samuel refuses all seven sons, saying of each, "The Lord has not chosen this one" (1 Sam 16:9). Samuel then turns to Jesse, "Are these all the children you have?" (16:11), for God had made plain to Samuel that in this house was, indeed, the second (but first true) king. Jesse responds, "Well, no, there's the youngest, who's out in the field, tending the sheep." "Fetch him," says Samuel. When the youth is brought in, Samuel sees David's beautiful face as inwardly God says to him, "Arise, anoint him: this is the one" (16:12).

I want to focus on a single aspect of this narrative: the status David holds in his father's house. It is plain that his seven powerful brothers, along with their lordly father, have reduced David to the merest of fieldworkers. So low is his status that Jesse, apparently, quite simply forgets David when Samuel—a figure of vast religious prestige in Israel—shows up to anoint a new king. We are invited by the narrative to imagine Jesse's moment of surprise, if not slight shock, when Samuel asks, "Are these all the children you have?" Oh, yes, yes, there *is* another one (but really, you know . . .). My point is this: In the very midst of David's being rejected by his family, God works salvation by raising up David through Samuel into kingship. All through Scripture, this same reality holds: the stone that was rejected becomes the cornerstone; the barren woman gives birth to the blessed child; the suffering servant heals the whole nation. The point is not that rejection *causes* worthiness. Rather, it is that rejection *reveals* the reality of genuine worth because worthiness is always rejected. In this familial rejection, the Davidic mind is revealed as possessing immense value.

The second moment immediately follows. When King Saul hears from his servants that Jesse has a son, David, skilled in playing the lyre, he calls the boy to his court. Now, Saul has been afflicted with a profound psychic derangement, for which his closest servants had prescribed the one solution that could reconstitute the wholeness of the king's psyche: let a man play the lyre when the psychosis is upon the king, and then he "shall be well" (16:16).

Introduction

David is brought before the king, and (just as Samuel did) Saul looks upon the face of David and immediately loves him so much that he grants him a great courtly honor: he makes David his armor-bearer, a role somewhat akin to being the personal secretary to a modern president. Saul then sends word to Jesse, asking the father that the son be permitted to come to the court not simply to take a prestigious job but, more deeply, to enter into a genuine relationship with the king: "And Saul sent to Jesse, saying, Let David, I beg you, stand before me: for he has found favor in my sight" (16:22). Then, within this relationship, one akin to an adoptive son to his adoptive father, David takes up the lyre when the king's derangement erupts in a psychotic episode: "David took the lyre and played it with his hand, so that Saul was refreshed and made well, and the evil spirit departed from him" (16:23).

The essential thing to note here is that this narrative explicitly connects psychological health and musical pattern. David's music *causes* Saul's healing because the music itself (the narrator tells us) is "with the Lord" (v. 18). David's music is therefore not self-performance. Rather, it is filled with the power to *ensoul* the listener. The verb used in v. 23—"Saul *was refreshed*"—carries in Hebrew the meaning of entering into a spacious openness, a place where one can now freely breathe. When, in the second century B.C., this verb was translated into Greek, the translators chose *anapsycho*, a lovely verb that means "to ascend up into one's soul." Saul regains his soul because David's music has this heavenly power to bring the listener up into that spacious place where one's soul can breathe freely and fully. Here, then, is what I am calling the second moment in the formation of David's mind: he actively practices the heavenly music wherein we become psychologically coherent. Thus ends the sixteenth chapter of First Samuel.

These first two moments of the Davidic mind—the revelation of worthiness through familial rejection and the creation of psychological coherence through music—may now be seen as themselves constituting an harmonic sequence. That is, the rejection and the music are as distinct from one another as any two notes in a musical sequence can be. Yet the sixteenth chapter establishes between them a finely persuasive harmony. The way the chapter does this is through a literary pattern termed *chiasmus*. In this pattern, the first and the final lines of a given biblical passage connect to one another; then the second line connects to the next-to-last line; then the third line connects to the third-to-last; and so on, until an exact midpoint is reached. Now, the *kind* of connection between each pair of lines varies immensely. Sometimes, the connection is direct repetition or simple parallelism; at other times, it is direct opposition. More often, the connection is one of intensification, with the second line in the chiastic pair in some way deepening the first, making it sharper and more drastic; and the intensification derives from, happens as a result of, emerges out of, the line at the center. Thus the pattern's midpoint provides a kind of pivot, one upon which the passage's entire significance may be seen to turn. Everything first flows toward this pivot; then everything flows out from it, changed in some way—transformed, indeed transfigured, without being at all "transcendentalized."

Chapter 16 of First Samuel possesses such a pattern. The first line mourns for Saul's psychic derangement; the final line (v. 23) exhibits Saul's psychic repatterning through David's music—the connection is straight opposition. The second line (v. 2) has Samuel fearfully telling God that Saul will discover the anointing of a new king at Jesse's house and then has God telling Samuel to use a sacrificial ritual to cover up the anointing from Saul. The second-to-last line has Saul sending a message to Jesse and asking him to give up—indeed to sacrifice—his son David for the court's and the king's sake. Here, the connection between this pair of lines is richly intensifying. That is, Samuel's cover-up in v. 2 succeeds so completely that Saul in v. 22 begs Jesse to send him the very person he would otherwise actively hate—and Saul begs in the voice of the one love that could (and, for a time, actually *will*) heal him, his love for David. In so doing, the second line (v. 22) simultaneously parallels and reverses, and thereby intensifies, the first line (v. 2). Thus, this connection makes manifest that operation which underlies all the Davidic narratives (indeed, all of Scripture): that invisible action wherein human persons freely choose what God—wholly unbeknownst to them—is willing for their redemption.

In this way, the chiastic pattern progresses through the whole sixteenth chapter, each verse sounding its own distinct note, yet each at the same time harmonically connecting to another. And as the narrative continues and the pattern unfolds, the contradictions grow ever sharper: David is rejected by his family, David is raised by his king; Saul is broken by psychosis, Saul is made well by music. What resolves the chapter's whole pattern is the single verse at the midpoint: "Arise, anoint him: this is the one" (v. 12). At this point, David is brought out from the darkness of his family's rejection to be anointed by God to become the light for all Israel. Then, from this point, David is made present to Saul as the bringer of musical light into the king's psychic darkness. Everything flows to this midpoint; and then everything flows from it. Its significance could not be clearer. All our sufferings and rejections are healed and reconciled in those actions wherein God gives Himself to us in the midst

Introduction

of our brokenness. Through David's music, Saul finds in the darkness of his psychotic depression a way back to God. Similarly, in the very midst of rejection, David is anointed by Samuel to be king through God's direct command. If the Davidic mind reveals its heavenly value in rejection, then it is given music for the divine healing of the broken world.

But in the next chapter (the seventeenth) of First Samuel, the mind of David achieves its third and perfective dimension: stillness. In his book *Leap Over a Wall*, Eugene H. Peterson beautifully describes the scene in the seventeenth chapter when David faces the Philistine giant, Goliath. At first, David follows Saul's urging to put on Saul's own armor. But then he sets aside the armor, saying, "I cannot use these, I have not tested them" (17:39). Then David steps over to the brook, to choose the stones for his sling. Peterson writes:

> My attention is caught and held by this wonderful but improbable scene: David on his knees at the brook; David kneeling and selecting five smooth stones, feeling each one, testing it for balance and size; David out in the middle of the valley of Elah—in full view of two armies, Philistine and Israelite, gathered on each side of the valley—kneeling at the brook, exposed and vulnerable. He's such a slight figure, this young shepherd. He's so unprotected. The air is heavy with hostility. There isn't a man on either side of the valley who isn't hefting a spear, sharpening a sword, getting ready to kill. The valley of Elah is a cauldron in which fear and hate and arrogance have been stirred and cooked for weeks into what's now a volatile and lethal brew. And David, seemingly oblivious to the danger, ignoring the spiked forest of spears and the glint of swords, kneels at the brook.[3]

Peterson has here supremely seen this astonishing moment. I want to emphasize what I call the *iconic* dimension in this scene: as David gazes down into the brook, he enters into what St. Isaac the Syrian calls *hesychia*, or *stillness*. In his magnificent *Ascetical Homilies* (seventh century A.D.), that greatest of Orthodox books on the teaching of prayer, St. Isaac defines stillness as "silence to all things," a word that in Syriac also means quietness, calmness, quiescence.[4] Amidst all the self-assertive yet terrified noise of all the violent restlessness, David simply, and entirely, *sets aside* the whole imminent catas-

---

3   Peterson, *Leap Over a Wall*, 35–36.
4   St. Isaac, *Ascetical Homilies*, 112, fn. 17.

Introduction

trophe, choosing instead to enter into this moment of silence and stillness. "It is ridiculous," says St. Isaac, "for us to speak of achieving stillness if we do not abandon all things and separate ourselves from every care."[5] As Peterson perceptively notes, David sets aside Saul's armor, "traveling light, delivered from an immense clutter"[6]—words that almost could come from a homily of St. Isaac's. And the mind's spins of anxiety are surely part of this clutter, for anxiety is the borrowed armor that the mind takes on in its desperate attempt to protect itself. As David kneels at the brook, Peterson imagines how the rippling water catches the sunlight and illumines David's breathtakingly beautiful face, now wholly concentrated in perfect stillness.

What expression do we see in David's face at this moment? I think we are to see every possible human expression, with every conceivable human emotion, all of them equally vividly present. That is, David's face is here perfectly *iconic* in just the same way Christ's face is in every true Orthodox icon. For what David's face, in this moment, beautifully holds is precisely what moves Saul to great love when he first sees David: the beauty of comprehensive stillness.

That is, stillness *is* every human expression all at once and perfectly in the same way that white is the presence of all color. Stillness is therefore what an entire life can come to express when a person learns to set aside (as David does here) every possible armor and to choose, instead, to love God. What we see here in David, then, is the understanding that stillness is a discipline. St. Isaac says: "learn what is the life of stillness, what is its work, what mysteries are concealed in this discipline."[7] This discipline is something as strong as a bronze spear and as light as a lyric poem—and strong partly because it is lyrical, and light partly because it is bronzen. In this way, the discipline of stillness can embrace and hold every conceivable aspect of the Davidic mind in the same way it can express every conceivable expression of the Davidic face.

In this way, the mind of David—ennobled in his family's rejection and strengthened in the graces of music—now gains its perfective purposiveness in stillness. Only as he kneels at the brook, in stillness, can David reconcile Jesse's dismissive indifference and Saul's prestigious elevation of him. But such reconciliation can never be achieved as mere cognitive process; it can only be achieved as an *actual practice actually lived*. The mind of David may thus be understood as that long discipline of stillness wherein the ruining

---

5   Ibid., 112.

6   Peterson, *Leap Over a Wall*, 42.

7   St. Isaac, *Ascetical Homilies*, 319.

oppositions of actual experience are held within the musical disciplines of lyric art: held, until God Himself can be seen in the very ruins themselves: seen, and felt, and overwhelmingly and gratefully loved. This overwhelming and grateful love *is* the mind of David.

It is also worth noting that these two chapters of First Samuel (16th and 17th) contain a brief passage that, for at least the past three centuries, scholarship has termed an anomaly, that is, a passage that makes no sense in narrative context. In the final four verses of the seventeenth chapter, Saul looks out over the scene of David triumphing over the Philistines after the slaying of Goliath. Saul turns to his field commander and asks, "Who is this boy?" (17:55). David is then brought to Saul. "Who are you, young man?" Saul asks. David answers, "I am the son of Jesse, your servant" (17:8).

What is going on? Why does Saul not know this boy whose singing has already healed him? Why is David introduced to Saul as if for the first time? How can this passage possibly fit into the narrative's forward movement?

In his book *The Art of Biblical Narrative*, Robert Alter offers a fine discussion of this particular anomaly. In our age of modern biblical scholarship, Alter holds, we have become so used to seeing biblical narratives as made up of disjunctive, misfitting "chunks" that we often fail to see exactly what the biblical authors were actually doing. For (Alter contends) in many of these sequences of misfitting chunks, the authors were actually employing a literary strategy not unlike contemporary cubism in painting. First, we are given one plane; then we have another; then a third; and so on. As in a cubist painting, these distinct planes of narrative touch one another but are not narratively integrated. Instead, the viewer negotiates the disjunctions by coming to see how each narrative plane is indispensable to the total meaning—but how no one plane can be subsumed into another one. The result is linear *dis-coherence* but spatial significance in a realm of total meaning. In such an approach, we can see this passage in First Samuel as one wherein Saul is saying: "I don't know you when you become a triumphant warrior, I know you and love you only as a lyric healer."

Read in this way, this narrative plane reveals a central dimension of the whole narrative's meaning. For, *on this plane alone*, we see the very heart of that chaotic blindness that is Saul's psychotic depression: he cannot see David whole. Put another way, Saul is here failing to see how David's invincibility as a warrior deeply informs—and is informed by—his skill as a lyricist, for the

xxxi

Introduction

bronze spear and the lyric poem are held together in the discipline of stillness. For Saul, David falls into two disjunct parts only one of which is comprehensible. Because of the narrative strategy, we are here not only seeing but also (to an interesting degree) *experiencing* Saul's blindness to David's wholeness. The very technique of prose narrative is thereby exhibiting the passage's meaning.

Thus, a great question opens before us. If the mind of David is formed in rejection, made coherent in music, and deepened in stillness, then what is the spiritual significance of psalmic technique? Or—to put the same question in the form we first asked it—how does the mind of David become in the Psalms the mind of Christ?

II.

There are three dimensions to the spiritual significance of psalmic technique. Now, every student of biblical poetics owes a great debt to Fr. John Breck's seminal book *The Shape of Biblical Language*. This work elucidates chiastic structures in biblical texts in ways both richly significant and immediately comprehensible. Chiasmus, says Breck, is that pattern which trains us "to read from the center outward and from the extremities toward the center."[8] So deep and widespread is the use of this pattern in all ancient literary cultures, Breck continues, that "writers in antiquity drew upon it almost instinctively."[9] Perhaps Breck's greatest insight into biblical chiastic pattern is his discussion of the pattern's double movement: (1) the movement from the passage's midpoint forward and back to its two extremities (i.e., its first and final lines), combined with (2) the movement from the passage's narrative start to its narrative conclusion. When these two movements are combined, the result is a situation wherein the forward narrative movement constantly *doubles back* to earlier points—but always at a higher, more intense, and more comprehensive level. Yet each doubling-back is necessarily *moving away* from the passage's midpoint; hence, each doubling-back can be seen to *ascend* from this midpoint. Equally, and at the same time, the movement toward this midpoint can be seen to *descend* toward it. These two distinct movements thus interlock and cohere.

Let us examine Psalm 66 to establish our bearings. Here is the text, slightly rearranged to emphasize the chiastic pattern:

---

8   Breck, *Biblical Language*, 29.
9   Ibid., 34.

> v. 1: God be merciful to us and bless us, and cause his face to shine upon us,
>> v. 2: That thy way may be known on earth, thy salvation among all nations.
>>> v. 3: Let the peoples praise thee, O God, let all the peoples praise thee.
>
> C (or v. 4): O let the nations be glad and sing for joy, for thou shalt judge the people righteously and govern the nations on earth.
>>> 3' (or v. 5): Let the peoples praise thee, O God, let all the peoples praise thee.
>> 2' (or v. 6): The earth has yielded her fruits; God, our own God, has blessed us.
> 1' (or v. 7): God has blessed us. Let all the ends of the earth be in fear of him.

The forward narrative movement in this lyric is quite plain to see: it begins with imploring God's blessing and ends with the fullest reality of that blessing having been received on earth. Equally plain is the psalm's midpoint center of significance: the lyricizing of our political life occurs when we let God govern the whole of our earthly life. Immediately around this midpoint is a pair of exactly repeating lines. But because the repeat line (3' or v. 5) occurs *after* the midpoint, the line gains an added intensity from it. Hence, this repeat line may be said to *ascend upward* from the center—while at the same moment it intersects with the *descending movement* of v. 3. These two movements thus interlock and cohere.

In the next pair of lines out from the center (vv. 2 and 2', or v. 6), the same interlocking occurs. The "salvation" that, in v. 2, God is implored to give becomes, in 2' (v. 6), the earth's agricultural bountifulness. Thus, the way of the heavenly God may be seen to descend upon the earth (in the psalm's first half) as the way (in the second half) of an actual fruitfulness of the fields. The result of such fruitfulness is that we can behold the very face of God shining upon us *in and through* our very awe and reverence of Him as He directly acts within the nation's political life. The significance of the psalm's double movement is therefore clear: as God descends into our actual life on earth, we ascend into actually beholding His face. The psalm catches and holds these two opposed movements in and as one clear lyric form.

Here, then, is the first dimension of psalmic technique: Chiastic patterning at once shapes and is shaped by the *experience of antinomy*. Now, this term

Introduction

antinomy seems first to have been used in classical Roman law to describe the circumstance of every jury trial: one side completely prosecutes while the other side entirely defends. According to all legal assumption, the truth can arise *only* through such jarring antinomical interaction. The philosophic use of the term begins with Immanuel Kant's *Critique of Pure Reason* (1781); and from Kant's work forward, the word exhibits a powerful and complex life.[10]

---

10   The term *antinomy* has been used in Orthodox theological discourse to describe "the affirmation of two contrasting or opposed truths, which cannot be reconciled on the level of the discursive reason although a reconciliation is possible on the higher level of contemplative experience . . . In order to reach out towards that which is inconceivable, the Christian tradition speaks in 'antinomic' fashion . . ." (Ware, 46). "If we exclude the antinomic dimension," Met. Kallistos continues, "the danger is that we shall never ascend to the level of spiritual understanding" (p. 51).

St. Gregory Palamas speaks of the divine nature in antinomic terms, in that it "must be called at the same time incommunicable and, in a sense communicable; we attain participation in the nature of God and yet he remains totally inaccessible. We must affirm both things at once and must preserve the antinomy as the criterion of piety" (Lossky, 26). Lossky goes on to say that "St. Gregory Palamas resolves this antinomy, without suppressing it, by preserving the deep-rooted mystery which dwells intact within the ineffable distinction between the essence (ousía) and its natural energies" (157).

Fr. Georges Florovsky critiques Lossky's understanding of the term in his response to Elder Sophrony Sakharov (who borrowed the concept from Lossky) concerning his "Theological Confession": "The antinomic character of dogmas is undeniable. But there also remains the question of the transformation of the reason [*razum*]. For the divine Logos is no antinomy which undermines the "logical"; rather, here is *the full measure of Logos*. Thus, antinomy in theology (first announced in Russian theology by Fr. P. Florensky) always bothers me, even in Lossky. Last, 'antinomy' lies in the fact that the Divine Being is at once both meta-logical (because it transcends created reason) and totally non-logical (because creaturely 'reason' itself is only an 'image' of the divine Logos). Antinomy is removed in 'contemplation': *theoria*—*henosis* [union]. In any case, the Divine Being is neither a-logical nor paralogical, and hence theological knowledge (the *gnosis* of John the Theologian) can not be a-logical ('irrational') or paralogical. Even antinomy is not paralogism. The holy Fathers clearly distinguish between *hyper* [above, beyond] and *para* [against]" (Florovsky to Sakharov, 78–79). That is, while

Introduction

Antinomicalness is, above everything else, an *experience*. It is the experience of disjunction, the experience wherein human discursive rationality breaks helplessly apart in the face of—better, *in the teeth of*—dissonant, often harsh realities. Such realities are the very ground of all biblical (indeed, all *human*) experience. The agony of forced exile is, at the same moment, the way of redemptive joy; the created world is simultaneously completely good, completely fallen, and completely redeemed; Christ is at once fully divine and fully human. There is no direct way wherein human reason alone can reconcile the disjunctive elements in these experiences; equally, there is no way whereby any element can be eliminated without radically falsifying the experience. Our fallen rationality simply breaks down when it directly confronts such antinomies as these. And chiastic pattern in the Psalms is thus the literary structure that most perfectly fits the experience of antinomy. For the contrastive structure firmly and directly holds all of antinomy's jarring contradictions.

But psalmic antinomy has a deeper significance: it contains its own reconciliations. The mind of David is continually broken on the reefs of all the world's most dreadful antinomies. Psalm 87 says: "Thy furies have swept through me, thy terrors have utterly unmade me" (v. 16). I am overwhelmed with terror and fury; and yet I am blessed, because God—the "God of my salvation" (v. 1)—is Himself steering the agony: *"thy* furies" and *"thy* terrors." What merely human rationality could even survive, let alone master, such antinomy? The rational mind thus breaks. Yet once so broken—and it is broken in the action of every psalm—the mind of David can then be *lyricized by God*—enlarged, made new, illumined, by David's love for God and God's for him. Now, amidst the very brokenness, he can begin to sing that wholeness and healing which God Himself is singing: "O Lord, thou shalt open my lips and my mouth shall declare thy praise" (Ps 50:15). By singing the psalm, the Davidic mind heals itself and all the world.

Nevertheless, though the salvific mind of David can teach, praise, and love God, it cannot (as will the mind of Christ in the Gospels) finally *comprehend* God. The line in the Psalms between genuinely loving and fully knowing God is the thinnest and finest line imaginable. So thin and so fine is it that here, at this line, we may see how the mind of David begins, through the chiastic art of lyric antinomy, to become indeed the mind of Christ. For the Davidic mind becomes so open to God that it draws near to becoming

> knowledge of God may be, according to a certain definition, supra-rational, it is not irrational, and may (according to a wider definition of reason) be rightly called "rational."—Ed.

Introduction

divinized in the very intimacy. In this first dimension of psalmic technique, then, through the chiastic patterning of antinomical experience, the mind of David draws close to God in deepest love.

The second dimension of significance to psalmic technique arises from the first: the dimension of *blessedness*. St. Gregory of Nyssa sees the "aim of the entire Psalter in the first word of the Book of Psalms":[11] "*Blessed* is the man who walks not in the counsel of the ungodly." The Greek word used by the Septuagint to translate the Hebrew is *makarios*. As the Psalter proceeds, each of the successive sixty-two occurrences of blessedness gathers in all the prior experiences, deepening and intensifying the entire significance of blessedness. For the whole Psalter unfolds in the very same fashion every psalm does: in antinomical movements within chiastic patterns. And as it does, the antinomies grow always sharper and more dire as the mind of David continues to grow correspondingly more illumined in blessedness.

This way toward the experience of blessedness is beautifully registered in the longest psalm, LXX 118, which gives us in its first stanza: "I shall keep Thy statutes; do not utterly forsake me" (v. 8). As we move through the 176 lines of this poem, we see affirmed the truth that God never has and never will utterly abandon anyone, *never*. He is always moving toward us in every way possible. What is necessary is that we move also and always toward Him. The psalmist must take his own steps in the dance—keeping God's statutes, turning to God in prayer—in order to meet God already coming toward him, not forsaking him, never having forsaken him. Watch now how the pattern of the dance moves through these lines:

> Blessed art thou, O Lord,
> Teach me thy statutes. (v. 12)
> I am a stranger on the earth,
> Hide not thy commandments from me. (v. 19)
> My soul lies prostrate on the earth,
> Quicken me according to thy word. (v. 25)
> I declared my ways, and thou didst hear me,
> Teach me thy statutes. (v. 26)
> My soul has fainted from depression,
> Strengthen me with thy words. (v. 28)
> I have clung to thy testimonies,
> O Lord, put me not to shame. (v. 31)
> Behold, I have longed for thy commandments,

---

[11] Heine, *Treatise*, 12.

> Quicken me in thy righteousness. (v. 40)

This pattern by no means exhausts what is going on in this complex psalm, but it defines a basic step in the dance of relation with God. We move in our lives, we turn that movement toward God, we enter into intimate relation with Him through prayer, and we find that He is always already moving toward us to carry us up into His dance of salvation. But we must make these first movements ourselves in order to know and experience this. It is not enough to remain prostrate on the ground, fainted from depression, alien on the earth, or even to cling to His testimonies or long for His commandments; we must take the next step of inviting Him into intimate relationship with us through prayer. And when we do, we find ourselves already quickened, strengthened, taught. In the tradition of the Orthodox Church, this turning toward God is called in Greek *metanoia*, which means the turning-around of consciousness, translated in English by the word *repentance*. We turn to face God, right where we are, even in the midst of our tears of pain and self-pity, and He receives us into His dance and transfigures us. This is blessednesss.

The third dimension of psalmic technique gathers in the first two and becomes their shared ground. For as the mind of David draws near to God, first in love and then in blessedness, psalmic technique then reveals its most perfective dimension: the dimension of *memory*. In its antinomical movements throughout the Psalter, the mind of David *remembers* and *is remembered by* the active presence of God. Yet this deepening of memory is never, in the Psalms, a simple straight line. For now, in Psalm 17, David sees God face to face; then, in Psalm 87, he grieves God's total abandonment of him. Yet such intimacies and abandonments are both grounded in the rocksolid depths of ineradicable memory. Thus, psalmic memory exhibits a *double movement*: (1) we remember and forget God in a kind of inescapable eddying into and out of each psalm's center; and (2) we are remembered by Him in an irreversible movement running straight from our birth and into our death and then beyond. The fulfillment of all desires in the Psalms occurs always as perfect memory: "I shall never forget thy statutes, in them thou hast quickened me to life" (118:93)—a line that is the chiastic center of Psalm 118. The essential connection is here plain: to *not forget God* is to *be quickened by Him*; that is, to be given actual life—as the baby in the womb is "quickened"—is the direct function of psalmic memory. In this way, memory may be best understood as the generative, or creative, principle of all psalmic thought.

Such are some of the spiritual significances of psalmic technique. And thus such are the movements whereby the mind of David draws near to the

Introduction

mind of Christ, is always *becoming* the mind of Christ. Such generative process of transformation in the Psalms has this essential property: the mind of Christ *fulfills* the mind of David, but it never overwhelms it, never uses it up or casts it aside. In other words, Christ as Messiah does not employ the Davidic mind as instrument. Instead, the mind of Christ unceasingly *remembers* the Davidic mind, thereby holding David in eternal memory in the fullness of his personhood.

Thus, the relation of Christ to David is, in Psalms, a *kenotic* relationship, for just beyond the Psalms is the cross of Christ.[12] Every Davidic kenosis is made full, is *remembered*, by Christ in His death and resurrection. This action of memory is most powerfully registered in the Gospels when Christ dies on the cross with the first line of Psalm 21 on His lips: "O God, my God, hear me: Why hast thou forsaken me?" The chiastic center of Psalm 21 says: "they have pierced my hands and my feet" (v. 16) in the violence of the crucifixion. Everything in Psalm 21 thus descends into this center and then arises from it. The result is the characteristic double movement of psalmic patterning: (1) the God-forsakenness of v. 1 moves straightforwardly toward the God-fulfillment of v. 31, an unswerving line of lyric narrative. At the same time (2), both the initial forsakenness and the final fulfillment gain full significance only in their descending-ascending movements into and out of the psalm's center. As a result of the double movement, the mockery of v. 8—"Let [God] save him since he delights in [God]"—is chiastically answered in v. 24: "When I cried to Him, [God] heard." Thus, in dying in and through this terrifying psalm, Christ thereby *remembers* and *fulfills* every Davidic action of psalmic kenosis. He gives Himself completely on the cross in order that David (and every one of us) may thereby in the Psalms completely live.

In the sixth century A.D., Cassiodorus composed in Latin his luminous commentary on the entire Psalter. In his preface, he quotes a passage from St. Athanasius about (says Cassiodorus) "the peculiar nature of the Psalter":

> Whoever recites the words of a psalm seems to be repeating his own words, to be singing in solitude words of a psalm composed by himself; it does not seem to be another speaking or explaining what he takes up and reads. It is as though he were speaking from his own person, such is the nature of the words he utters. He seems to be expressing the kind of language used as if spoken from the heart. He seems to offer words to God.[13]

12 *Kenotic*, from the Greek *kenosis*, means 'self-emptying.' See xvii, n. 4.

13 Cassiodorus, *Explanation*, 41.

St. Athanasius here perfectly expresses the experience of probably every reader of Psalms: the experience of intimacy. As experience, every act of intimacy is, at first, an experience of *shock*. At one moment, a person is far from you; the next instant, that person is immensely close, and vivid, and actual. Systemic shock is one's entry into real intimacy. St. Athanasius is saying that the systemic shock of the Psalms is so great that their words actually become, for every one of us, our own most intimate words. We are *fully in* the mind of the other and yet, in the very same instant, the other remains *fully operative on* us. In this way, psalmic intimacy is fundamentally an experience of antinomy, an experience wherein every psalm seems to declare the words of Christ Himself when He says to the Father: "I in them, and Thou in Me, that they may be made perfect in one" (John 17:23). The effects of psalmic intimacy are therefore vast beyond all our reckonings.

As the psalmist enters into and moves within his lyric dance with God, the calamities, actual and potential, of his life are carefully woven into a close-up intimacy of relation with God that is the beginning of his salvation. For let us remember that the divine partner in this dance of incorruption is always Christ; He it is who changed not a jot or tittle of the Law but perfectly fulfilled it. The psalmist's world doesn't get any better as he turns all of his experience toward God—the world's corruption will go on until the end of time and likely get worse. What changes is he himself. How he changes is *toward the grace of incorruption*, toward acquiring the very mind of Christ. It is into this that each one of us is called in every line of Psalms, where, with David, we find ourselves cast down in our supposed strengths only to be raised up in our real weaknesses.

The chiastic pattern of each psalm is thus an icon of God's relation to us; and each movement of descent and ascent perfectly reflects our own ceaseless turnings away from and toward Him. If we seek to dance instead a solo, in pursuit of some ruling passion of our own, we will find ourselves in a dance of entropy descending into depression and death. God will not invade the freedom He has given us in order to turn us from this. Yet He will take each heartfelt cry as an invitation for Him to enter our dance and transform our solo terrors into blessedness. This dance is one that grows always in beauty and grace as, with David, we allow His mind to become our own.

To read Psalms is to learn the way to this Grace.

THE PSALMS OF DAVID

KATHISMA ONE

PSALM 1
A psalm of David.

BLESSED IS THE MAN who walks not in the counsel of the ungodly, nor takes the way of the sinful, nor sits in the seat of the scornful.
2 But his will is in the law of the Lord and in his law he will meditate day and night.
3 And he shall be like a tree whose fruit comes forth in its season and whose leaf shall not wither, and whatever he does shall flourish.
4 Not so are the ungodly, not so, but they are like the chaff the wind drives from the face of the earth.

5 Therefore the ungodly shall not rise in the judgment nor the sinful in the counsel of the righteous.
6 For the Lord knows the way of the righteous and the way of the ungodly shall perish.

PSALM 2
A psalm of David.

WHY DO THE nations rage and the people meditate vain things? 2 The kings of the earth set themselves, and the rulers take counsel together against the Lord and against his Christ, saying: *Selah*
3 Let us break their bonds in pieces and cast away their yoke from us.
4 He who sits in the heavens shall laugh at them, the Lord shall hold them in derision.
5 Then shall he speak to them in his wrath and distress them in his deep displeasure.
6 Yet I have been set as king by him over his holy hill of Zion, declaring his decree.
7 The Lord has said to me: Thou art my Son, today I have begotten thee,
8 Ask of me, and I will give thee the nations for thine inheritance and the ends of the earth for thy possession.
9 Thou shalt shepherd them with an iron staff, thou shalt shatter them like a potter's vessel.
10 And now, O kings, be wise; be instructed, all you judges of the earth.
11 Serve the Lord with fear and rejoice in him with trembling.
12 Seize hold of his teaching lest he be angry with you and you perish from the righteous way when his fury shall blaze up quickly. Blessed are all they that put their trust in him.

PSALM 3
A psalm of David,
when he fled in the desert from his son Absalom.

LORD, WHY DO they that afflict me keep multiplying? Many are they that rise up against me.

Kathisma One

2 Many are they who say to my soul: There is no salvation for him in his God. *Selah*

3 But thou, O Lord, art my protector, my glory and the one who lifts up my head.

4 I cried to the Lord with my voice and he heard me from his holy hill. *Selah*

5 I lay down and slept; I awoke, for the Lord will protect me.

6 I will not be afraid of ten thousands of people who set themselves against me all around.

7 Arise, O Lord, save me, O my God, for thou hast struck all those who are my enemies without cause, thou hast broken the teeth of the sinners.

8 Salvation is from the Lord and thy blessing is upon thy people.

Glory. Both now. Alleluia.*

PSALM 4
For the end of the struggle, a psalmic hymn of David†

THOU HAST HEARD me when I called, O God of my righteousness, thou hast opened my heart when I was in distress; have mercy on me and hear my prayer.

2 How long, O you sons of men, will you be slow of heart? Why do you love vain things and seek after lies? *Selah*

3 Know that the Lord has made his holy one wondrous; the Lord will hear me when I cry out to him.

4 Have anger, but do not sin, commune with your own heart on your bed and become still in your sorrow. *Selah*

5 Offer the sacrifice of righteousness and put your trust in the Lord.

6 There are many who say: Who will show us good things? Lord, the light of thy countenance has been signed upon us.

---

* These are the opening words of several short prayers recited at the end of each stasis of the Psalter. See p. 176 for their complete text.

† The phrase "of the struggle" is adduced from St. Gregory of Nyssa, who says "the term 'end' [is meant] to heighten the eagerness in those who are contending by means of virtues in the stadium of life." The "end of the struggle" implies a victory over evil. Heine, *Treatise*.

7   Thou hast put gladness in my heart; from a season of wheat, wine and oil they have multiplied.
8   I will lie down in peace and sleep comes at once, for thou alone, Lord, hast made me dwell in hope.

PSALM 5
For the end of the struggle, a psalm of David for the one receiving the inheritance.

Give ear to my words, O Lord, understand my outcry.
2   Give heed to the voice of my cry, my King and my God, for to thee will I pray, O Lord.
3   In the morning thou shalt hear my voice, O Lord; in the morning I will stand before thee and thou shalt behold me.
4   For thou art not a God who takes pleasure in wickedness, nor shall the evildoer dwell with thee.
5   The transgressors shall not stand in thy sight; thou hatest all the workers of iniquity.
6   Thou shalt destroy all those that speak lies; the Lord abhors the man of violence and deceit.
7   But as for me, I will come into thy house in the fullness of thy mercy, in fear of thee I will worship toward thy holy temple.
8   Lead me, O Lord, in thy righteousness because of my enemies, make straight thy way before me.
9   For there is no truth in their mouth, their heart is an empty thing, their throat is an open grave, they lie with their tongues.
10 Judge them, O God, let them fall by their own counsels, cast them out in the multitude of their transgressions, for they have provoked thee, O Lord.
11 But let all those that put their trust in thee rejoice; forever they will shout for joy, for thou wilt dwell in them, and all those that love thy name will glory in thee, for thou wilt bless the righteous.
12 O Lord, thou hast crowned us with the shield of thy good will.

PSALM 6

For the end of the struggle,
a psalmic hymn of David for the eighth day.

O LORD, DO NOT reprove me in thine anger nor discipline me in thy wrath.
2. Have mercy on me, O Lord, for I am sick; O Lord, heal me, for my bones are troubled
3. And my soul is greatly troubled; but thou, O Lord—how long?
4. Turn again, O Lord, and deliver my soul, O save me for thy mercy's sake,
5. For in death there is no remembrance of thee, in the grave who will sing praises to thee?
6. I am weary with my groaning, all night I will make my bed swim, I will drench my couch with my tears.
7. My eye is troubled by anger, I grow old among all my enemies.
8. Depart from me, all you workers of iniquity, for the Lord has heard the voice of my weeping,
9. The Lord has heard my supplication, the Lord has received my prayer.
10. Let all my enemies be ashamed and greatly troubled, let them turn back and be ashamed suddenly.

Glory. Both now. Alleluia.

PSALM 7

A psalm of David, which he sang to the Lord
concerning the words of Cush, son of Benjamin.

O LORD MY GOD, in thee have I hoped, save me from all my accusers and deliver me,
2. Lest like lions they tear apart my soul while there is none to redeem or save.
3. O Lord my God, if I have done this, if there is iniquity in my hands,
4. If I have dealt back evil to those dealing evil to me, let me fall empty from my enemies' hands,
5. Let the enemy pursue my soul and overtake it, trampling my life to the ground, making my glory settle in the dust.   *Selah*

6 Arise, O Lord, in thine anger, be exalted to the very boundaries of my enemies; awaken, O Lord, in the decree thou hast ordained,
7 And the congregation of the peoples shall surround thee; for their sakes return on high.
8 The Lord shall judge the people; judge me, O Lord, according to my righteousness and according to my integrity within me.
9 O make an end to the wickedness of sinners and establish the just, for God tests to the depths of the heart.
10 My righteous defense is from God, who saves the upright in heart.
11 God is a judge just, strong and patient, not raining down anger every day.
12 If you do not turn back he will polish up his sword; he has strung his bow and readied it,
13 And he has readied his instruments of death, arrows fashioned for the accusers' hot rage.
14 Behold, the wicked labored with injustice, he conceived pain and brought forth wickedness,
15 He opened up a pit and dug it out, and he will fall into the ditch he has made.
16 The pain shall return on his own head, the injustice shall crash down on his scalp.
17 I will sing praise to the Lord in accordance with his righteousness and will sing to the name of the Lord most high.

PSALM 8

*For the end of the struggle,
a psalm of David concerning the wine-presses.*

O Lord, our Lord, how wondrous is thy name in all the earth, for thy splendor is exalted far beyond the heavens.
2 From the mouths of babes and nursing infants thou hast brought forth perfect praise because of thine enemies, that thou mayest silence enemy and avenger.
3 For I shall look at the heavens, the works of thy fingers, the moon and stars that thou hast established.
4 What is man that thou rememberest him, or the son of man that thou comest to him?

5 For thou hast made him a little lower than the angels, and thou hast crowned him with glory and honor.
6 Thou hast made him to rule over the works of thy hands, thou hast put all things under his feet,
7 All sheep and oxen—even the beasts of the field,
8 The birds of the heavens and the fish of the sea and all things passing through the paths of the sea.
9 O Lord, our Lord, how wondrous is thy name in all the earth.

Glory. Both now. Alleluia.

KATHISMA TWO

PSALM 9
*For the end of the struggle,
a psalm of David concerning
the hidden things of the Son.*

I WILL PRAISE THEE, O LORD, with my whole heart, I will tell of all thy wondrous works.
2 I will be glad and rejoice in thee, I will sing praise to thy name, O Most High.
3 When my enemies turn back, they shall fall and perish before thy face.
4 For thou upholdest my right and my cause, thou sittest enthroned, judging in righteousness.

5 Thou rebukest the nations, thou destroyest the wicked, blotting out their name for ever and ever.
6 The enemy's swords are completely destroyed and thou hast laid waste their cities, even their memory fell with a resounding crash.
7 But the Lord endures forever; he has prepared his throne for the judgment.
8 He shall judge the whole world in righteousness, he shall judge all peoples in uprightness.
9 The Lord is also a refuge for the poor, safe haven in the seasons of trouble.
10 And those who know thy name put their trust in thee, for thou, Lord, forsakest not them that need thee.
11 Sing to the Lord who dwells in Zion, proclaim his ways of living to his people,
12 For in avenging bloody deeds, he remembers them, he does not forget the cry of the humble.
13 Have mercy on me, O Lord, see how I have been humbled by my enemies, thou who liftest me up from the gates of death
14 That I may proclaim all thy praises in the gates of Zion's daughter. I will rejoice in thy salvation.
15 The nations are trapped in the corruption they made; in the net that they hid, their own foot is caught.
16 The Lord is known in the judgments he executes, the wicked is snared in the works of his own hands.   *Selah*
17 Let the wicked be turned away into hell, all nations that keep forgetting God.
18 For the poor man shall not be forgotten in the end, the patience of the paupers shall not perish forever.
19 Arise, O Lord, do not let man prevail; let the nations be judged in thy sight.
20 Set a lawgiver over them, O Lord, that the nations may know themselves to be but men.   *Selah*
21 Why dost thou stand afar off, O Lord? Why dost thou look away in seasons of trouble?
22 In the wicked man's arrogance, the poor are set afire; let him be caught in the schemes he himself devises.
23 For the wicked man sings praise to the lusts of his soul, and the unjust man praises himself.

24 The wicked man provokes the Lord, thinking that God will not fully execute his wrath; for God is not in all his thoughts.
25 His ways are corrupt in every season; thy judgments are far beyond his sight; he smashes down all his enemies.
26 For he has said in his heart: I shall never be shaken, for generations and generations I shall be well.
27 His cursing mouth is filled with lies and bitterness, his tongue deals out pain and grief.
28 He waits in ambush with the wealthy to murder the innocent in secret places, his eyes fixed upon the poor,
29 He lies in wait secretly, like a lion in his den; he lies in wait to seize upon the poor, seizing the poor man by drawing him in.
30 In setting his trap, he bows humbly down that the poor man may fall into his power.
31 For he said in his heart: God always forgets, hiding his face so as never to see it.
32 Arise, O Lord God, let thy hand be lifted high, and do not forget thy poor ones.
33 Why has the unholy man provoked God? Saying in his heart: Thou wilt never call me to account for this.
34 But thou dost see; thou knowest the depth of pain and outrage and takest them into thy hands; and so the poor man gives himself over to thee, thou art always the helper of the orphaned.
35 Break the arm of the wicked and the evil man, his sinfulness rooted out until it withers away.
36 The Lord will reign always, unto ages of ages; and, O nations, you will perish from his earth.
37 The Lord has heard the yearning of the poor; the readying of their hearts thine ear has heeded,
38 To do justice to the orphaned and humbled, that no one may again speak violence on earth.

PSALM 10

For the end of the struggle, a psalm of David.

IN THE LORD I trust—how can you say to my soul: Flee to the mountains like a sparrow.

2 See: The wicked bend their bow, readying their arrow on the string, that on some dark, moonless night they may shoot down the upright in heart.
3 What thou hast created, they destroy. What can the righteous man do?
4 The Lord is in his holy temple, the Lord's throne is in heaven, his eyes are fixed upon the poor, his eyelids closely watch the sons of men.
5 The Lord closely watches both righteous and wicked, but he who loves violence hates his own soul.
6 Upon the wicked he will rain down snares; fire and brimstone and a raging wind shall be the portion of their cup.
7 The righteous Lord loves righteousness, his countenance beholds the upright.

Glory. Both now. Alleluia.

PSALM 11
*For the end of the struggle,
a psalm of David for the eighth day.*

SAVE ME, O Lord, for the devout are no more, the truthful vanish from among the sons of men,
2 They speak idly every one with his neighbor, with flattering lips and double heart they speak.
3 Let the Lord destroy all flattering lips and the tongue that speaks proud things
4 And those saying: We will magnify our own tongues, our lips are our own; who is Lord over us?
5 For the oppression of the poor, for the sighing of the needy, now will I arise, says the Lord; I will set them in salvation, I will be manifest in it.
6 The words of the Lord are pure words, like silver fired in a furnace of earth, purified seven times.
7 Thou shalt protect us, O Lord, thou shalt preserve us from this generation forever.
8 The wicked prowl in circles everywhere; in thy loftiness thou carest greatly for the sons of men.

The Psalms of David

PSALM 12
For the end of the struggle, a psalm of David.

How long, O Lord? Wilt thou forget me forever? How long wilt thou hide thy face from me?
2. When can I put an end to my soul's endless plans, having terror in my heart every day? How long will my enemy be exalted over me?
3. Look down and hear me, O Lord my God, enlighten my eyes, lest I sleep the sleep of death,
4. Lest my enemy say: I have prevailed against him. For my persecutors delight when I am shaken.
5. But I have trusted in thy mercy, my heart shall rejoice in thy salvation.
6. I will sing to the Lord who has dealt bountifully with me, I will sing praise to the name of the Lord most high.

PSALM 13
For the end of the struggle, a psalm of David.

The fool says in his heart: There is no God. They are corrupt, they do abominable deeds, there is none, not even one, who does good.
2. The Lord looks down from heaven upon the sons of men to see if there are any that understand and seek God.
3. They have all turned aside, altogether corrupted; there is none, not even one, who does good.
4. Do all the workers of wickedness know nothing at all? They eat up my people as they eat bread and do not call on the Lord.
5. They were in great fear where no fear was, for God is in the generation of the righteous.
6. The poor man's plan you treat with contempt because the Lord is his hope.
7. Who will give out of Zion the salvation of Israel? When the Lord brings back the captivity of his people, let Jacob rejoice, let Israel be glad.

Glory. Both now. Alleluia.

PSALM 14
A psalm of David.

LORD, WHO SHALL abide in thy tabernacle? Who shall dwell in thy holy mountain?
2. He who walks uprightly, working righteousness, speaking the truth in his heart,
3. Not backbiting with his tongue, nor doing evil to his neighbor, nor blaming those closest to him.
4. He counts as nothing those doing wickedness, but he glorifies those fearing the Lord. The one who keeps faith with his neighbor,
5. Not lending money in order to gain interest, nor taking bribes against the innocent: The one doing these things shall never be shaken.

PSALM 15
An inscription of David.

PRESERVE ME, O Lord, for in thee do I hope.
2. I say to the Lord: Thou art my Lord, thou hast no need of my good things.
3. In the saints who are on his earth, in them he has made wondrous all his will,
4. Their sickness worsening who have rushed to other gods. I will not join in those assemblies of blood, I will not have those names on my lips.
5. The Lord is the portion of my inheritance and my cup; thou restorest my inheritance to me.
6. Portions of the fine places are given to me, my inheritance is the very finest.
7. I will bless the Lord who lets me understand; my heart also instructs me in the night seasons.
8. I see the Lord always before me; because he is at my right hand, I shall never be shaken.
9. Therefore my heart is glad, my tongue rejoices, my flesh shall also dwell in hope.
10. For thou wilt not abandon my soul to Hades, nor suffer thy holy one to see corruption.

11 Thou makest known to me life's ways, thou wilt fill me in joy with thy countenance, at thy right hand are pleasures forevermore.

PSALM 16
A prayer of David.

Hear me, O Lord of my righteousness, attend to my supplication, give ear to my prayer free from deceit.
2 From thy countenance let my vindication come, let my eyes behold uprightness.
3 Thou hast tested my heart, visiting in the night, thou hast tried me and found nothing unjust.
4 To keep my mouth from the talk of men's deeds, through the words of thy lips I held to hard ways.
5 Restore my steps in thy paths that my footsteps may not slip.
6 I have called upon thee, for thou hast listened, O God; incline thine ear to me and hear my speech.
7 Show forth thy wondrous mercy, saving them that hope in thee from those who rise against thy right hand.
8 Keep me as the apple of thine eye; in the shelter of thy wings thou wilt shelter me
9 From the unholy faces afflicting me, from the deadly enemies surrounding my soul.
10 They are enclosed in their own fat, with their mouth they speak proudly.
11 Casting me out, they have now surrounded me, inclining their eyes down to the earth,
12 Like a lion ready to tear its prey, like a young lion lurking in secret places.
13 Arise, O Lord, outrun them, cast them down, deliver my soul from the wicked, thy sword from the enemies of thy hand.
14 Lord, separate thy few from the earth, even in their lifetimes. And those whose belly was filled with thy treasures like their swine were satisfied and left the remnants to their children.
15 As for me, in righteousness I shall behold thy countenance, I shall be satisfied in beholding thy glory.

Glory. Both now. Alleluia.

KATHISMA THREE

PSALM 17
*For the end of the struggle, for David,
the servant of God, when he addressed the Lord
with the words of this ode,
on the day the Lord delivered him
from the hands of all his enemies,
and from Saul's hands,
and he said:*

I WILL LOVE THEE, O LORD, my strength.
2   The Lord is my strength, my refuge, my deliverer, my God is my helper, on him I will hope, my shield, the horn of my salvation, my protector.
3   Praising, I will call upon the Lord and from my enemies I shall be saved.
4   The agonies of death surrounded me, the floods of wickedness terrified me,

5. The agonies of Hades encircled me, the snares of death ran me down.
6. Afflicted, I called upon the Lord, I cried out to my God; he heard my voice from his holy temple, my cry shall come before him, straight into his ears.
7. Then the earth was shaken into trembling, the foundations of mountains began to rock and shake in his anger with them.
8. Smoke rose up in his wrath, fire burst raging from his countenance, setting coals alight.
9. He bowed the heavens also, and came down with darkness under his feet.
10. And he rode upon a cherub, and flew, he flew upon the wings of the wind.
11. He made darkness his secret place, his tabernacle was around him, dark water in the sky's clouds.
12. At the brightness before him, the clouds passed, hailstones and fiery coals.
13. The Lord thundered in the heavens, the Most High gave forth his voice,
14. And he sent forth his arrows, scattering them, multiplying lightnings in great disarray.
15. Then the springs of the sea were seen, the foundations of the world were uncovered by thy rebuke, O Lord, by the onbreathing spirit of thy wrath.
16. He sent from above, he took me, he drew me out of many waters.
17. He will deliver me from my strong enemy, from those hating me, for they were too strong for me.
18. They overran me in the day of my affliction, but the Lord became my support
19. And he led me into spaciousness, he will deliver me because he delights in me.
20. The Lord will reward me according to my righteousness, according to the purity of my hands will he recompense me,
21. For I have kept the ways of the Lord and have not wickedly departed from my God.
22. For all his judgments are before me, and I have not put away his statutes from me.

23 I will also be blameless before him, I will keep myself from my iniquity.
24 The Lord will recompense me according to my righteousness, according to the purity of my hands before his eyes.
25 With the merciful thou wilt be merciful, with the innocent man thou wilt be innocent;
26 With the elect thou wilt be elect, with the twisted thou wilt be twisted.
27 For thou wilt save a humble people and thou wilt humble the eyes of the arrogant.
28 For thou wilt light my lamp, O Lord, O my God, thou wilt light my darkness.
29 For in thee I shall be set free from raiding gangs, in my God I shall leap over a wall.
30 O my God—blameless is his way, the words of the Lord are tried in fire, shield to all who set their hope in him.
31 For who is a god, except the Lord? And who is a god, except our God?
32 It is God who is arming me with power and has made my way blameless.
33 He makes my feet like the feet of deer and sets me on my high places,
34 Teaching my hands to make war; and thou makest my arms a bronze bow.
35 Thou hast given me the shield of thy salvation, thy right hand has upheld me, thy teaching guides me forever, thy gentleness has made me great.
36 Thou hast enlarged my path under me so that my feet did not slip.
37 I shall pursue my enemies and overtake them, I shall not turn back until they are destroyed.
38 I shall wound them until they cannot rise, they shall fall under my feet.
39 For thou hast armed me with strength for the battle, thou hast subdued under me those who rose up against me.
40 Thou hast given me the necks of my enemies, all those hating me thou hast destroyed.
41 They cried out, but there was none to save—even to the Lord, but he did not answer them.

42 I will grind them to dust blowing in the wind, I will cast them out like dirt in the street.
43 Deliver me from the strivings of the people, make me the head of nations: A people I never knew have served me,
44 The moment they heard they obeyed me; sons who are strangers have lied to me,
45 Sons who are strangers have faded away, and, trembling, have strayed from their paths.
46 The Lord lives, and blessed be my God. Let the salvation of my God be exalted,
47 The God who is avenging me, who is subduing the peoples under me,
48 Who is my deliverer from my enemies' rage. From those rising against me thou wilt exalt me, from the violent man thou wilt set me free.
49 Therefore I will give thanks to thee, O Lord, among the nations, and sing praises to thy name.
50 Great deliverance he gives to his king, and shows mercy to his Christ, to David and his descendants forevermore.

Glory. Both now. Alleluia.

PSALM 18

For the end of the struggle, a psalm of David.

THE HEAVENS DECLARE the glory of God, the firmament shows the works of his hands.
2 Day unto day utters speech and night unto night reveals knowledge.
3 There is no speech nor language where their voice is not heard.
4 Their voice has gone out through all the earth, their words to the ends of the world. He has set his tabernacle in the sun,
5 Which comes forth like a bridegroom from the bridal chamber, exulting like a strong man set to run the course.
6 Its rising is from one end of heaven, its circuit running to the other; nothing can hide from the heat of it.

7 The law of the Lord is perfect, converting the soul; the testimony of the Lord is sure, making children wise,
8 The statutes of the Lord are right, rejoicing the heart; the commandment of the Lord is pure, enlightening the eyes,
9 The fear of the Lord is clean, enduring forever; the judgments of the Lord are true and righteous altogether.
10 More to be desired are they than gold and precious stones, sweeter also than honey and the honeycomb.
11 For indeed thy servant keeps them, in keeping them there is great reward.
12 Who can understand his own transgressions? Cleanse me from secret faults; and from those of others spare thy servant.
13 If they have no dominion over me, then I shall be blameless and I shall be cleansed of great transgression.
14 The words of my mouth and my heart's meditation will be continually pleasing in thy presence, O Lord, my strength and my redeemer.

PSALM 19
For the end of the struggle, a psalm of David.

MAY THE LORD hear you in the day of affliction, may the name of the God of Jacob defend you.
2 May he send you help from the sanctuary, and from Zion may he help you.
3 May he remember all your offerings, may your burnt sacrifice be honored.   *Selah*
4 May he give you according to your heart, may he fulfill all your plans.
5 We will rejoice in thy salvation, and in the name of our God we will glory. May the Lord fulfill all your petitions.
6 Now I know that the Lord saves his Christ; he will answer him from his holy heaven, in the dominion of his right hand is salvation.
7 Some glory in chariots, some in horses, but in the name of our Lord God we shall be glorified.
8 They were shackled and have fallen, but we have risen and stand upright.

9 O Lord, save thy king and hear us in the day when we call.

PSALM 20
For the end of the struggle, a psalm of David.

THE KING SHALL joy in thy strength, O Lord, and in thy salvation how greatly shall he rejoice.
2 Thou hast given him his soul's desire, not withholding the request of his lips.　　Selah
3 For thou hast gone before him with blessings of goodness, thou hast set a crown of precious stones on his head.
4 He asked life of thee, and thou gavest it him—length of days for ever and ever.
5 Great is his glory in thy salvation; glory and majesty thou shalt place upon him.
6 For thou shalt make him most blessed forever, filling him with the joy of thy countenance.
7 For the king hopes in the Lord, and in the mercy of the Most High he will not be shaken.
8 May thy hand be found on all thine enemies, thy right hand on those who hate thee.
9 Thou shalt make them a fiery furnace in the revelation of thy countenance, the Lord in his wrath shall swallow them, the fire shall devour them.
10 Their offspring thou shalt destroy from the earth, their descendants from among the sons of men.
11 For they bent all their evils against thee, they devised a plot they cannot uphold,
12 For thou shalt make them turn their back; among thy remnant thou shalt make ready their countenance.
13 Be exalted, O Lord, in thine own strength. We will sing and praise thy power.

Glory. Both now. Alleluia.

PSALM 21

*For the end of the struggle, a psalm of David
concerning the help that comes in the morning.*

O GOD, MY GOD, hear me: Why hast thou forsaken me? So far from saving me are my roaring words.
2. O my God, all day I cry out to thee and Thou dost not hear me; all night, and I do no wrong in this.
3. Thou dwellest in the sanctuary, O praise of Israel.
4. Our fathers hoped in thee, they hoped in thee and thou didst deliver them.
5. They cried to thee and they were saved, they hoped in thee and were not disgraced.
6. But I am a worm, and no man; a reproach of men and despised by the people.
7. All those who see me ridicule me, their lips babbling, their heads wagging:
8. He hoped in the Lord, let him rescue him, let him save him since he delights in him.
9. For thou art he that drew me out from the womb, my hope from my mother's breast,
10. I was cast upon thee from the womb, from my mother's womb thou art my God.
11. Do not stand off from me, for affliction is near and there is no one to help.
12. Many young bulls have surrounded me, fat bulls have encircled me.
13. They open wide their mouths against me, like a raging and roaring lion.
14. I am poured out like water, my bones are all scattered, my heart is like wax melting into my stomach.
15. My strength is dried up like a potsherd, my tongue cleaves to my throat; thou hast led me into the dust of death.
16. For many dogs have surrounded me, a mob of evildoers has enclosed me, they have pierced my hands and my feet.
17. They number all my bones, they look and stare at me.
18. They divide my garments among them, and for my clothing they cast lots.
19. But, O Lord, do not take thy help from me, attend to my aid.

20 Free my soul from the sword, my only-begotten from the dog's hand;
21 Save me from the lion's mouth, my humility from the ox's horns.
22 I will declare thy name to my brethren, amidst the assembly I will sing to thee.
23 You who fear the Lord, praise him, all you descendants of Jacob, glorify him, and fear him, all you offspring of Israel.
24 For he has not despised nor scorned the beggar's plea, nor has he hid his face from me, and when I cried to him, he heard.
25 My praise is from thee in the great assembly, I will pay my vows before them that fear thee.
26 The poor shall eat and be satisfied, those who seek him will praise the Lord, their hearts will live forever.
27 All the ends of the world shall remember and turn to the Lord, and all families of the nations shall worship before thee,
28 For the kingdom is the Lord's, and he rules over the nations.
29 All the prosperous of the earth have eaten and worshiped; all those going down into the earth shall bow down before him. My soul lives on in him.
30 And my seed shall serve him, the coming generation shall be told of the Lord
31 And they will declare his righteousness to a people who will be born, whom the Lord has made.

PSALM 22
A psalm of David.

The Lord is my shepherd, I shall not want.
2 In green pastures he makes me a home, he nourishes me beside the still water.
3 He uplifts my soul, he leads me in the paths of righteousness for his name's sake.
4 Though I walk in the shadow of death, I will fear no evil, for thou art with me, thy rod and thy staff, they comfort me.
5 Thou preparest me a table in my persecutors' presence, thou anointest my head with oil, and the cup thou givest me to drink— how supremely good it is!
6 And thy mercy shall pursue me all the days of my life, and I shall dwell in the Lord's house for the length of my days.

PSALM 23

*A psalm of David,
concerning the first day of the week.*

The earth is the Lord's, and all its fullness, the whole world and all who dwell in it.
2. For he has founded it upon the seas and established it upon the waters.
3. Who shall ascend the mountain of the Lord? Who shall stand in his holy place?
4. He who has clean hands and a pure heart, who has not driven his soul unto vanity, who has not sworn falsely to his neighbor.
5. He shall receive blessing from the Lord, great mercy from the God of his salvation.
6. This is the generation of those who seek him, who seek the face of Jacob's God.   *Selah*
7. Raise up the gates, O you princes, and be uplifted, you everlasting doors, the King of glory shall come in.
8. Who is this King of glory? The Lord strong and mighty, the Lord mighty in battle.
9. Raise up the gates, O you princes, and be uplifted, you everlasting doors, and the King of glory shall come in.
10. Who is this King of glory? The Lord of hosts, he is the King of glory.

Glory. Both now. Alleluia.

KATHISMA FOUR

PSALM 24
A psalm of David.

O THEE, O LORD, I lift up my soul.
 2 O my God, I trust in thee, let me not be put to shame, let not my enemies laugh at me.
 3 For all who wait upon thee shall never be put to shame; let those be ashamed who work wickedness.
 4 Make known thy ways to me, O Lord, and teach me thy paths.
 5 Lead me in thy truth and teach me, for thou art the God of my salvation, on thee I wait all the day.
 6 Remember thy compassion, O Lord, and thy mercy, for they are from of old.

7. Do not remember the sins of my youth, nor my ignorance, but remember me according to thy mercy, because of thy lovingkindness, O Lord.
8. Merciful and upright is the Lord, therefore he will establish the law to guide sinners in the way.
9. The gentle he will guide in justice, the meek he will teach his ways.
10. All the ways of the Lord are mercy and truth for those seeking his covenant and his testimonies.
11. For thy name's sake, O Lord, pardon my iniquity, for it is great.
12. Who is the man that fears the Lord? Him shall God teach in the way he has chosen.
13. His soul shall dwell amidst good things, his seed shall inherit the earth.
14. The Lord is the strength of those who fear him, and he will show them his covenant.
15. My eyes are ever toward the Lord, for he shall pluck my feet out of the net.
16. Look upon me and have mercy on me, for I am an only child and poor.
17. My heart's afflictions have multiplied, bring me out of my distresses.
18. Look on my lowliness and my pain, and forgive all my sins.
19. Look on my enemies, they have multiplied, they hate me with unjustified hatred.
20. Keep my soul and deliver me, let me not be put to shame, for I put my hope in thee.
21. The innocent and the upright cleave to me, for I wait upon thee.
22. Redeem Israel, O God, out of all his troubles.

PSALM 25
David's.

JUDGE ME, O Lord, for I have walked in my innocence; hoping in the Lord, I shall not weaken.
2. Prove me, O Lord, and test me; purify my mind and my heart.
3. For thy mercy is before my eyes and I have delighted in thy truth.
4. I have not sat down with vain councils, nor will I go in with those that transgress the law.

5   I have hated the assembly of evildoers and will not sit with the wicked.
6   I will wash my hands in innocence, so I will go about thine altar, O Lord,
7   That I may hear the voice of thy praise and tell of all thy wondrous works.
8   Lord, I have loved the splendor of thy house, the place where thy glory dwells.
9   Do not destroy my soul with the sinful, nor my life with bloodthirsty men
10 In whose hands are iniquities, whose right hand is full of bribes.
11 But as for me, I have walked in my innocence; redeem me and have mercy on me.
12 For my foot stands in uprightness; in the congregations I will bless thee, O Lord.

PSALM 26
David's, before his anointing.

The Lord is my light and my savior, whom shall I fear? The Lord is the defender of my life, what shall I dread?
2   When the wicked came to eat up my flesh, these enemies and foes of mine stumbled and fell.
3   Though an army come round about me, my heart shall not fear; though war be waged against me, still shall I have hope.
4   One thing I asked of the Lord, seeking this: that I may dwell in the Lord's house all the days of my life, beholding the delights of the Lord and visiting his holy temple.
5   For he hid me in his tabernacle in the day of my troubles, he sheltered me in the secret place of his tabernacle, he set me high upon a rock.
6   And now, behold, he has lifted up my head above my enemies all around me; I went around and offered sacrifices of joy in his tabernacle; I will sing praises of melody to the Lord.
7   Hear my voice, O Lord, when I cry, have mercy on me and hear me.
8   My heart said: I will seek thee, O Lord; thy face, Lord, I will seek.

9   Do not hide thy face from me, do not turn away from thy servant in anger; be my helper, do not leave me nor forsake me, O God my savior.
10 When my father and my mother forsook me, then the Lord took me up.
11 Guide me, O Lord, in the way of thy law, set me on the straight path because of my enemies.
12 Do not deliver me to my adversaries' will, for false witnesses have risen against me and their injustice lies even to itself.
13 I believe I shall see the Lord's goodness in the land of the living.
14 Wait on the Lord and take courage and strengthen your heart; wait, I say, on the Lord.

Glory. Both now. Alleluia.

PSALM 27
David's.

To thee, O Lord, I cry out: Be not silent to me; no, be never silent to me, lest I become like those who go down into the pit.
2   Hear the voice of my supplication in my praying to thee, in the lifting up of my hands toward thy holy temple.
3   Do not draw my soul off with the wicked, do not destroy me with the workers of iniquity, who speak peace to their neighbors, but evil is in their hearts.
4   Give them according to their deeds, according to the wickedness of their works. Give them according to the work of their hands, give back to them their due reward.
5   Because they do not comprehend the works of the Lord, nor the acts of his hands, thou shalt destroy them and never rebuild them.
6   Blessed be the Lord, because he has heard the voice of my supplications.
7   The Lord is my helper and my defender, in him my heart hopes and I am helped, and my whole flesh flourishes; with my whole will I shall confess him.
8   The Lord is their strength, and he is the saving refuge of his Christ.

9 Save thy people and bless thine inheritance, shepherd them also, and bear them up forever.

PSALM 28
*A psalm of David,
a processional of the tabernacle.*

Give unto the Lord, O you sons of God, give unto the Lord glory and honor.
2 Give unto the Lord the glory due his name, worship the Lord in his holy court.
3 The voice of the Lord is upon the waters, the God of glory thunders, the Lord is upon the many waters.
4 The voice of the Lord is powerful, the voice of the Lord is full of majesty.
5 The voice of the Lord who shatters cedars, the Lord shall shatter the cedars of Lebanon,
6 He shall grind them like the calf, Lebanon, but his beloved shall be like the unicorn's young.
7 The voice of the Lord cutting through fiery flames,
8 The Lord's voice making the desert shake; the Lord shall shake the desert of Kadesh.
9 The Lord's voice brings the deer to birthgiving, and it strips bare the forest, and all in his temple give glory.
10 The Lord will dwell in the deluge, the Lord shall sit as King forever.
11 The Lord will give strength to his people, the Lord will bless his people with peace.

PSALM 29
*For the end of the struggle,
a psalm sung for the dedication of the house of David.*

I will exalt thee, O Lord, for thou hast upheld me, not letting my foes rejoice over me.
2 O Lord my God, I cried out to thee and thou didst heal me.
3 O Lord, thou hast led my soul out of Hades, thou hast saved me from those going down to the pit.

4 Sing praises to the Lord, you saints of his, and give thanks at the memory of his holiness.
5 For rage is in his anger, but in his will there is life; in evening, the weeping sets in, but great joy comes in the morning.
6 As for me, I said in my prosperity I shall never be shaken.
7 Lord, by thy will thou gavest strength to my beauty; thou didst hide thy countenance and I was troubled.
8 I shall cry out to thee, O Lord, to the Lord I shall make supplication:
9 What profit is there in my blood when I go down to the pit? Will the dust praise thee? Will it declare thy truth?
10 The Lord heard and had mercy on me, the Lord became my helper.
11 Thou hast turned my lamentation to joy, tearing up my sackcloth and clothing me in gladness
12 That my glory may sing praise to thee, that I not be stunned with sadness. O Lord my God, I will give thanks to thee forever.

Glory. Both now. Alleluia.

PSALM 30
For the end of the struggle,
a psalm of David in a time of terror.

In thee, O Lord, I have hoped, may I never be ashamed; in thy righteousness, deliver and rescue me.
2 Bow down thine ear to me, deliver me speedily; be a God who defends me, a house of refuge to save me.
3 For thou art my strength and my refuge, and for thy name's sake thou wilt guide me and nourish me.
4 For thou wilt set me free from this snare they have hid for me, for thou, O Lord, art my defender.
5 Into thy hands I shall commit my spirit; thou hast redeemed me, O Lord God of truth.
6 Thou hast hated those who guard fiercely their emptiness, but I have hoped in the Lord.
7 I will be glad and rejoice in thy mercy, for thou hast beheld my lowliness, thou hast saved my soul from anguish

8 And didst not imprison me in my enemy's hands; thou hast set my feet in a wide place.
9 Have mercy on me, O Lord, for I am afflicted, my eye is vexed by fury, so are my soul and my stomach.
10 For my life is wasted with grief and my years with groaning, my strength is weakened with poverty, my very bones are vexed.
11 I am the scorn of all my enemies and especially of all my neighbors, I strike fear in all my acquaintances, those seeing me outside all flee from me.
12 I am forgotten as a dead man, out of mind, I am like a broken vessel.
13 For I hear the blame of those who dwell close all around me; when they gather together against me, they scheme to take away my life.
14 But as for me, I have hoped in thee, O Lord; I said: Thou art my God.
15 My times are in thy hands, deliver me from the hand of my enemies and from those who persecute me.
16 Make thy countenance shine upon thy servant, save me in thy mercy.
17 Lead me not into disgrace, O Lord, for I have called upon thee; let the ungodly be disgraced, lead them down into Hades.
18 Let lying lips be put to silence in speaking evil against the righteous with arrogant contempt.
19 How great is thy lovingkindness, O Lord, which thou didst hide for those who fear thee, which thou hast wrought for those who hope in thee in the presence of the sons of men.
20 Thou shalt secretly hide them in thy countenance away from men's schemings, thou shalt shelter them in thy tabernacle from the strife of tongues.
21 Blessed be the Lord, for he has made wondrous his mercy in a city under siege.
22 But I had said in my terror, I am cut off, cut off from thy sight— therefore thou didst hear the voice of my prayer when I cried out to thee.
23 O love the Lord, all you his saints, for the Lord seeks out the truth, and those who act in great arrogance he repays in full.

24 Be of good courage and let your heart be strengthened, all you who hope in the Lord.

PSALM 31
David's, concerning instruction.

BLESSED ARE THOSE whose iniquities are forgiven, whose sins are covered.
2 Blessed is the man whose sin the Lord does not reckon, in whose mouth is no deceit.
3 Because I kept silent, my bones grew old through my groaning all the day long.
4 For day and night thy hand was heavy upon me, I was turned into agony when the thorn pierced me.   *Selah*
5 I confessed my sin, my iniquity I have not hidden, saying: Before the Lord I will confess iniquity against myself. And thou forgavest my heart's unholiness.   *Selah*
6 For this reason, every devout man will pray to thee at set times and seasons; when the floods of great waters come they will not reach him.
7 Thou art my refuge from the afflictions that encircle me, O my Joy! redeem me from those closing in on me.   *Selah*
8 I will give thee understanding, I will teach thee this road to walk, I will hold fast my eyes on thee.
9 Do not be like the horse or the mule, which have no understanding, which must be harnessed with bit and bridle else they will not come near thee.
10 Many are the scourges of the sinner, but mercy shall encircle him who hopes in the Lord.
11 Be glad in the Lord and rejoice, you righteous, and shout for joy, all you upright in heart.

Glory. Both now. Alleluia.

KATHISMA FIVE

PSALM 32
David's, untitled among the Hebrews.

REJOICE IN THE LORD, O you righteous, praise befits the upright.
2 Praise the Lord with the lyre, make music to him on a ten-string harp.
3 Sing to him a new song, chant beautifully to him in jubilation.
4 For the word of the Lord is true and all his works are done in faith.
5 He loves mercy and judgment, the earth is filled with the Lord's mercy.

6 By the Lord's word were the heavens made firm, all their hosts by the breath of his mouth,
7 Gathering the seawaters up as into a wineskin, putting the deeps down into storehouses.
8 Let all the earth fear the Lord, let all the world's inhabitants be shaken by him.
9 For he spoke and they came into being, he commanded and they were created.
10 The Lord scatters the counsels of nations, he makes men's thoughts become as nothing, he makes as nothing the counsels of kings.
11 The counsel of the Lord stands forever, the thoughts of his heart unto all generations.
12 Blessed is the nation whose God is the Lord, the people he has chosen as his own inheritance.
13 The Lord looks down from heaven, he sees all the sons of men.
14 From the place he has made to dwell, he looks out upon all the earth's peoples,
15 He who alone has fashioned their hearts, who comprehends all their works.
16 A king is not saved by his strong army nor a giant by his immense strength;
17 A horse is a vain hope for safety, nor shall its great strength deliver him.
18 Behold, the eye of the Lord is on those who fear him, on those who hope in his mercy,
19 To deliver their soul from death and to keep them alive in famine.
20 Our soul shall wait for the Lord, he is our helper and defender.
21 For our heart shall rejoice in him because we have hoped in his holy name.
22 Let thy mercy, O Lord, be upon us, as we have set our hope on thee.

PSALM 33
*David's, when he changed his appearance
before Abimilech, who let him go, and he went away.*

I will bless the Lord at all times, his praise shall continually be in my mouth.

2 My soul shall be praised in the Lord, the meek shall hear of it and be glad.

3 O magnify the Lord with me and let us exalt his name together.

4 I sought the Lord and he heard me, and delivered me from all my afflictions.

5 Come close to him and be illumined, and your countenance shall never be shamed.

6 This poor man cried out and the Lord heard him, and saved him out of all his troubles.

7 The angel of the Lord shall encamp around those who fear him, and deliver them.

8 O taste and see that the Lord is good; blessed is the man who puts his hope in him.

9 Fear the Lord, you his saints, there is no want to those who fear him.

10 Rich men have turned poor and starved, but those seeking the Lord shall not lack any good things.

11 Come, children, listen to me, I will teach you the fear of the Lord.

12 Who is the man who desires life, who loves to behold good days?

13 Keep your tongue from evil and your lips from speaking deceit.

14 Depart from evil and do good; seek peace and pursue it.

15 The eyes of the Lord are on the righteous, his ears are open to their supplications.

16 The Lord's countenance is upon evildoers, to uproot their remembrance from the earth.

17 The righteous cry out and the Lord hears and delivers them out of all their troubles.

18 The Lord is near those shattered in heart, the humbled in spirit he will save.

19 Many are the troubles of the righteous, but the Lord delivers them out of them all.

20 The Lord shall guard all their bones, not one of them shall be broken.

21 The death of sinners is evil, and those hating the righteous shall go wrong.
22 The Lord will redeem the souls of his servants and none will go wrong who put their hope in him.

Glory. Both now. Alleluia.

PSALM 34
David's.

Judge, O Lord, those judging me, make war on those who war against me.
2 Lay hold of weapon and shield and rise up for my help.
3 Draw forth the sword and stop those who pursue me; say to my soul: I am thy salvation.
4 May those seeking out my soul be ashamed and dishonored, may those plotting evil against me be turned back and confounded.
5 May they be like chaff in the wind's face, an angel of the Lord afflicting them.
6 May their way be dark and slippery, an angel of the Lord pursuing them.
7 For without cause they have hidden their snare of corruption for me, for no reason they have reviled my soul.
8 May a snare catch him up unaware, may the trap he has set catch him up, may he fall into his very own trap.
9 And my soul shall be joyful in the Lord, it shall rejoice in his salvation.
10 All my bones shall say: Lord, Lord, who is like thee, delivering the poor from hands stronger than he, the poor and needy from those wrecking him.
11 Unjust witnesses rose up against me, asking me things I knew nothing about.
12 They repaid me evil for good, and desolation for my soul.
13 But I, when they assailed me, I put on sackcloth, I humbled my soul with fasting, my prayer would return to my heart.
14 As if he were friend, as if our brother, I would seek to please; like one mourning and saddened, I would be humbled.

15 But they rejoiced in gathering against me; scourges gathered against me and I did not know it, and even when they scattered, they still did not cease;
16 They kept heaping contempt on me, they kept tearing me with their teeth.
17 Lord, when wilt thou look on this? Rescue my soul from their malice, my only-begotten from the lions.
18 I will confess thee in the great assembly, I will praise thee amidst a mighty people.
19 Let them not rejoice over me who are unjustly my enemies, nor let them wink with the eye who hate me without cause.
20 For they spoke peace to me, but in their wrath they schemed
21 And opened wide their mouths at me, saying: Yes, yes! With our own eyes we saw it.
22 But thou, O Lord, hast seen this, do not keep silence. O Lord, do not be far from me.
23 Arise, O Lord, attend to my cause; my God and my Lord, vindicate me.
24 Judge me, O Lord, my God, according to thy righteousness, and let them not rejoice against me.
25 Let them not say in their hearts: Yes, yes! Our soul's desire! We have swallowed him up!
26 Let those who rejoice at my woes be ashamed and confounded together, let those shouting contempt at me be clothed with shame and confusion.
27 Let those desiring my righteous cause shout for joy and be glad, saying over and over: May the Lord be magnified who desires His servant's peace.
28 And my tongue shall speak of thy righteousness and of thy praise all the day long.

PSALM 35

For the end of the struggle, concerning David, the servant of the Lord.

THE TRANSGRESSOR, that he may sin, says within himself there is no fear of God before his eyes.
2 For he has woven lies all around himself so as not to see his own evil and hate it.

3 The words of his mouth are wickedness and deceit, he has chosen not to understand doing good.
4 He devises wickedness on his bed, he sets himself in a way that is not good, he does not abhor evil.
5 Thy mercy, O Lord, is in the heavens, thy truth reaches even to the clouds.
6 Thy righteousness is like the mountains of God, thy judgment is a great deep; O Lord, thou wilt save man and beast.
7 Thou hast multiplied thy mercy, O God. The sons of men shall have hope beneath the shelter of thy wings.
8 They shall be drunk on the richness of thy house, thou wilt have them drink deeply from the torrents of thy delights.
9 For with thee is the fountain of life, in thy light we shall see light.
10 O continue thy mercy to those who know thee, thy righteousness to the upright in heart.
11 Let not the foot of pride come against me, let not the sinner's hand move me.
12 There the workers of iniquity have fallen, they are cast down and now cannot stand.

Glory. Both now. Alleluia.

PSALM 36
David's.

Do not be moved to jealousy by evildoers, do not envy the workers of iniquity.
2 For like grass shall they swiftly die, like green herbs shall they swiftly wither.
3 Hope in the Lord and be gracious, dwell in the land and you will be tended by its riches.
4 Delight yourself also in the Lord and he shall give you the desires of your heart.
5 Reveal your way to the Lord, set your hope in him and he shall bring it to pass.
6 He shall bring forth your righteousness as light, your justice as the noonday sun.

The Psalms of David

7. Submit to the Lord and supplicate him; never envy him who prospers in his way nor the one successful in wicked schemes.
8. Cease from anger and forsake wrath, do not let envy lead to evil deeds.
9. For evildoers shall be cut off, but those who wait on the Lord shall inherit the earth.
10. For in a little while the evildoer shall perish, you shall look for his place but not find it.
11. But the meek shall inherit the earth, taking delight in the fullness of peace.
12. The sinner shall sharply watch the just man, gnashing at him with his teeth.
13. But the Lord shall laugh at him, foreseeing that his day will come.
14. The wicked have drawn the sword and have bent their bow to cast down the poor and needy, to slay the upright in heart.
15. May their sword enter their own heart, may their bows be shattered.
16. Better the little that the just man has than the great riches of the sinner.
17. For the arms of the wicked shall be broken, but the Lord upholds the righteous.
18. The Lord knows the ways of the blameless and their inheritance shall be forever.
19. They shall not be disgraced in an evil time, in days of famine they shall be filled.
20. But the wicked shall perish, the Lord's enemies shall vanish when they glorify and exalt themselves; like smoke they shall vanish away.
21. The sinner borrows and will never repay, the righteous shows mercy and gives.
22. For those blessing him shall inherit the earth, those cursing him shall utterly perish.
23. The Lord rightly directs a man's steps; and he shall delight in his way.
24. When he stumbles, he shall not be cast down, for the Lord upholds him with his hand.
25. Once I was young, now I am old, yet I have not seen the righteous forsaken nor his children begging bread.

26. Day in and day out, he is merciful and lends, and his children shall be blessed.
27. Depart from evil and do good, and dwell forevermore.
28. For the Lord loves judgment and will never forsake his saints; they shall be kept safe forever. But the children of the ungodly shall be utterly destroyed.
29. The righteous shall inherit the earth and dwell in it forever.
30. The mouth of the righteous shall speak wisdom, his tongue talk of judgment.
31. The law of God is in his heart, none of his steps shall stumble.
32. The wicked watches the righteous and seeks to slay him.
33. The Lord will not leave him in his hands nor condemn at all when he judges him.
34. Wait on the Lord, endure patiently his way, and he will exalt you to inherit the earth; you shall see the sinners utterly destroyed.
35. I have seen the ungodly greatly exalted, lifting himself up like the cedars of Lebanon.
36. Yet I passed by and, behold, he was no more, I sought him out but his place could not be found.
37. Preserve innocence, be witness to uprightness, for such is what remains for the peaceful.
38. But the transgressors shall be utterly destroyed, what remains for the ungodly is utter destruction.
39. But the Lord is the salvation of the righteous, their defender in times of affliction.
40. And the Lord shall help them and deliver them, he shall deliver them from sinners and save them because they have hoped in him.

Glory. Both now. Alleluia.

KATHISMA SIX

PSALM 37
*A psalm of David,
for the remembering of the Sabbath.*

LORD, DO NOT REBUKE ME in thy wrath nor chasten me in thine anger.

2 For thine arrows have stuck fast in me, thy hand lies heavily on me.
3 My flesh has no healing in the face of thine anger, my bones have no peace in the face of my sins.
4 For my iniquities have gone over my head, like a heavy burden they are too heavy for me.
5 My wounds grow foul and fester in the face of my foolishness.

6 I was troubled, I was bowed down greatly, I went mourning all the day long.
7 For my loins are filled with mockeries, there is no healing in my flesh.
8 I am afflicted and greatly humbled, I have roared from my heart's groanings.
9 Lord, all my desire is before thee, my groaning is not hidden from thee.
10 My heart is troubled, my strength fails, even the light of my eyes is gone from me.
11 Friends and neighbors drew up against me, those closest to me stood afar off.
12 Those seeking my soul took to violence, those seeking evil for me spoke emptiness, plotting deception all the day long.
13 But like a deaf man, I did not hear; like a mute, I never opened my mouth.
14 I became like a man who never hears, in whose mouth there is never rebuke.
15 For in thee, O Lord, I have hoped; thou wilt hear me, O Lord my God.
16 I said: Let not my enemies rejoice over me; when I slip, they speak great boasts against me.
17 For I am ready for scourges, my sorrow is continually before me.
18 For I will declare my iniquity, I will be in anguish over my sin.
19 But my enemies flourish and have grown strong over me; those hating me unjustly have multiplied.
20 Those dealing me evil for good have slandered me for doing good, casting my love away like a foul corpse.
21 Do not forsake me, O Lord; O my God, be not far from me.
22 Make haste to help me, O Lord, my salvation.

PSALM 38

For the end of the struggle, an ode of David to Jeduthun.

I SAID: I WILL guard my ways lest I sin with my tongue; I set a guard on my mouth when sinners set themselves against me.
2 I was mute in humble silence, I held my peace even from good, and my sorrow was stirred.

3   My heart was hot within me and in my musings fires will burn. Then I spoke with my tongue:
4   Lord, make me to know my end and what is the measure of my days, that I may know how few I have.
5   Behold, thou hast made my days a handbreadth, my whole being is nothing before thee. But all is vanity, every living man.   *Selah*
6   Like a shadow indeed a man goes about, vainly indeed they are troubled, he heaps up treasure and does not know for whom he will gather it.
7   And now who is my patience? Is it not the Lord? My whole being is from thee.
8   Deliver me from all my transgressions; thou hast made me the reproach of the fool.
9   I was mute, I did not open my mouth, for thou art the one who created me.
10 Take away thy scourges from me, from thy hand I have fainted away.
11 With rebukes thou chastenest man's iniquity, sweeping his soul away like spider webs; vainly indeed are all men troubled.   *Selah*
12 Hear my prayer, O Lord, and give ear to my cry; do not be silent at my tears, for I am a stranger with thee, a sojourner, as all my fathers were.
13 Spare me that I may revive before I go away and am no more.

PSALM 39

For the end of the struggle, a psalm of David.

I waited patiently for the Lord and he inclined to me and heard my supplication.
2   He has led me up out of misery's pit, away from the miry mud; he has set my feet on firm ground and has directed my steps.
3   He has put a new song in my mouth, a hymn to our God. Many shall see and fear and shall hope in the Lord.
4   Blessed is the man whose hope is in the name of the Lord, who has not gazed into vain emptiness and crazed lies.
5   Many, O Lord my God, are thy wonders that thou hast created, and in all these thy thoughts no one has likeness to thee; I spoke out and said: They are more than can be numbered.

6 Sacrifice and offering thou didst not desire, but thou hast prepared a body for me; burnt offering and oblation thou didst not require.
7 Then I said: Behold, I come (as is written of me in the scroll of the book)
8 Delighting to do thy will, O my God, for thy law is in the midst of my heart.
9 I gladly proclaimed righteousness in the great congregation; yes, I shall never restrain my lips, O Lord, indeed thou knowest this.
10 I did not hide thy righteousness in my heart, I declared thy truth and thy salvation, I did not hide thy mercy and thy truth from the great congregation.
11 Do not, O Lord, take thy compassion from me; may thy mercy and truth forever preserve me.
12 For countless evils have surrounded me, my iniquities so took hold of me that I could not see; they have multiplied more than the hairs of my head, and all heart has gone from me.
13 Be pleased, O Lord, to deliver me; O Lord, make haste to help me.
14 May those seeking to shatter my soul be disgraced and ever confounded; may those wishing evil for me be turned back and confounded.
15 May those mocking: Well done, well done! be given disgrace as their prize.
16 But may all those seeking thee, O Lord, rejoice and be glad in thee; may those loving thy salvation ceaselessly say: The Lord be magnified!
17 As for me, I am poor and needy, the Lord will care for me. Thou art my help and my deliverer; do not delay, O my God.

Glory. Both now. Alleluia.

PSALM 40
For the end of the struggle, a psalm of David.

BLESSED IS THE one who understands the poor man and the needy one; the Lord will deliver him in an evil day.
2 May the Lord keep him and quicken him and make him blessed on the earth, not giving him over to his enemies' hands.

3   May the Lord help him on his bed of pain; in his sickness, thou hast made his whole bed.
4   I said: Lord, have mercy on me, heal my soul, for I have sinned against thee.
5   My enemies spoke evil of me: When will he die and his name perish?
6   When he came in to visit he spoke lies, his heart gathered iniquity to itself; when he went out he spoke it.
7   All my enemies whisper against me, against me they devise evils for me.
8   They speak treacherous words about me: Now that he sleeps, will he wake again?
9   Even the peaceful man in whom I hoped, even the one eating my bread has dealt wicked treachery to me.
10 Do thou, O Lord, have mercy on me and raise me up, and I will repay them.
11 By this I know thou hast delighted in me: that my enemy has not rejoiced over me.
12 In my innocence thou hast upheld me and set me before thee forever.
13 Blessed be the Lord God of Israel from everlasting to everlasting. Amen and amen.

PSALM 41

For the end of the struggle,
a psalm of instruction for the sons of Korah.

As the deer longs for the water brooks, so my soul longs for thee, O my God.
2   My soul thirsts for God, for the living God. When shall I come and appear before the face of God?
3   My tears have been my bread day and night, while they say to me every day: Where is your God?
4   I remembered these things and poured out my soul within me, for I shall go into the wondrous tabernacle, even into the house of God, with a voice of rejoicing and praise, the voice of those keeping joyous feast day.

5 Why art thou cast down, O my soul? And why dost thou disquiet me? Hope in God, for I will give thanks to him. He is the salvation of my countenance and my God.
6 My soul within me is troubled, therefore I will remember thee from the land of Jordan and from Hermon's small mountain.
7 Deep calls to deep at the voice of thy cataracts, all thy waves and billows have gone over me.
8 By day the Lord will send his mercy; by night his song shall be with me, a prayer to the God of my life.
9 I will say to God: Thou art my protector, why hast thou forgotten me? Why must I go about all downcast in the afflictions of my enemies?
10 Breaking my bones, my enemies reproached me, saying every day: Where is your God?
11 Why art thou cast down, O my soul? And why dost thou disquiet me? Hope in God, for I will give thanks to him. He is the salvation of my countenance and my God.

PSALM 42
A psalm of David, untitled among the Hebrews.

JUDGE ME, O God, and defend my cause against an unholy nation; from the deceitful and unjust man deliver me.
2 For thou, O God, art my strength, why dost thou cast me off? Why must I go about downcast in the affliction of my enemies?
3 O send out thy light and thy truth, they have guided me and led me to thy holy mountain and to thy tabernacles.
4 Then I will come to the altar of God, the God who makes glad my youth, and on the harp I will praise thee, O God, my God.
5 Why art thou cast down, O my soul? And why dost thou disquiet me? Hope in God, for I will give thanks to him. He is the salvation of my countenance and my God.

Glory. Both now. Alleluia.

PSALM 43
A psalm of David, untitled among the Hebrews.

WE HAVE HEARD with our ears, O God, our fathers have told us what work thou didst in their days, in days of old.
2. Thy hand utterly destroyed the nations, planting them in their place, afflicting and casting out whole peoples.
3. For they inherited the land not by their own sword, nor did their own arm save them, but it was thy right hand and arm and the radiance of thy countenance, because thou hadst pleasure in them.
4. Thou art my very King and God, for thou dost command salvation for Jacob,
5. In thee we shall gore our enemies, and in thy name we shall grind down into nothing those rising up against us.
6. For I will not trust in my bow, nor shall my sword save me.
7. For thou hast saved us from our tormentors and disgraced those who hated us.
8. In God we shall be praised all day long, we shall exult in thy name forever.   *Selah*
9. But now thou hast rejected and disgraced us and wilt not go out with our armies.
10. Thou hast turned us back from our enemy, those hating us have plundered for themselves.
11. Thou hast given us up like sheep to be eaten, scattering us among the nations.
12. Thou hast sold thy people for next to nothing, and made no profit in selling them.
13. Thou hast made us our neighbors' reproach, a scorn and derision to those around us.
14. Thou hast made us a byword among the nations, a shaking of the head among the peoples.
15. All day long my disgrace is before me and the shame of my face has covered me
16. At the voice of him who blames and reviles, at the face of the enemy and persecutor.
17. All this has come upon us but we have not forgotten thee, nor have we dealt falsely with thy covenant.
18. Our heart has not turned back, yet thou hast led our paths from thy way,

19 Thou hast humbled us in a place of affliction, and the shadow of death has covered us.
20 If we have forgotten the name of our God or stretched out our hands to a strange god
21 Would not God search this out? For he knows the secrets of the heart.
22 For thy sake we are killed all day long, we are reckoned as sheep for the slaughter.
23 Awake! Why dost thou sleep, O Lord? Arise! Do not cast us off forever.
24 Why dost thou turn away thy face and forget our poverty and affliction?
25 For our soul has been humbled to the dust, our belly has cleaved to the ground.
26 Arise, O Lord, for our help, and redeem us for thy name's sake.

PSALM 44

*For the end of the struggle, in alternating verses,
concerning instruction for the sons of Korah,
an ode about the Beloved.*

My heart has overflowed with a good word, I myself say my works to the king, my tongue is the pen of a swift-writing scribe.
2 Thou art fairer than the sons of men, grace has been poured on thy lips, therefore God has blessed thee forever.
3 Gird thy sword upon thy thigh, O mighty one, in thy splendor and thy beauty.
4 And string thy bow, prosper and reign because of truth, gentleness and righteousness, and wondrously shall thy right hand guide thee.
5 Thine arrows are sharp, O mighty one, in the heart of the king's enemies; the peoples shall fall under thee.
6 Thy throne, O God, is for ever and ever, thy royal scepter is a scepter of uprightness.
7 Thou hast loved righteousness and hated iniquity; therefore God, thy God, has anointed thee with the oil of gladness more than thy companions.

8   Myrrh and aloes and cassia exhale from thy garments, and from the ivory palaces they have gladdened thee,
9   These daughters of kings in thine honor. At thy right hand stood the queen dressed in gold-woven raiment richly embroidered.
10 Listen, O daughter, behold and incline thine ear: forget thine own people and thy father's house.
11 For the king shall greatly desire thy beauty, for he is himself thy Lord.
12 And the daughters of Tyre shall worship him with gifts, the rich among the people shall entreat thy countenance.
13 The king's daughter is all glorious within, her clothing is woven with gold.
14 The virgins who follow after her shall be brought to the king, those near her shall be brought to thee.
15 They shall be brought with gladness and rejoicing, they shall enter into the king's palace.
16 In place of thy fathers are sons born to thee, whom thou shalt make princes over all the earth.
17 I will make thy name to be remembered from generation to generation; all peoples shall give praise to thee unto ages of ages, forever.

PSALM 45

For the end of the struggle, a psalm of David concerning hidden things, for the sons of Korah.

God is our refuge and strength, helper in the afflictions so assailing us.
2   Therefore we will not fear when the earth is shaken, when the mountains are carried down into the sea's depths.
3   Their waters roared and were troubled, the mountains were troubled by his might.   *Selah*
4   The river's rushings gladden God's city, the Most High has hallowed his tabernacle.
5   God is in the midst of her, she shall never be shaken; God shall help her even before the dawn comes.
6   The nations were troubled, kingdoms fell; he uttered his voice, and the earth shook.

7 The Lord of hosts is with us, the God of Jacob is our protector. *Selah*
8 Come, behold the works of the Lord, the wonders he has wrought on earth,
9 Making wars cease on all the earth—for he will break the bow, shatter the weapons, he will burn up the shields in fire.
10 Be still, and know that I am God; I will be exalted among the nations, I will be exalted in the earth.
11 The Lord of hosts is with us, the God of Jacob is our protector.

Glory. Both now. Alleluia.

KATHISMA SEVEN

PSALM 46
*For the end of the struggle,
a psalm concerning the sons of Korah.*

CLAP YOUR HANDS, all you nations, shout to God with the voice of rejoicing,

2 For the Lord Most High is fearsome, a great King over all the earth.

3 He has subdued the peoples under us and the nations under our feet.

4 He has chosen us for his inheritance, the beauty of Jacob, which he loved.   *Selah*

5 God has gone up with a shout, the Lord with the sound of a trumpet.
6 Sing praises to God, sing praises, sing praises to our King, sing praises,
7 For God is the King of all the earth, sing praises with understanding.
8 God reigns over the nations, God sits on his holy throne.
9 The princes of the people have gathered together with the God of Abraham, for the mighty ones of God are greatly exalted.

PSALM 47

A Psalmic Ode concerning the Sons of Korah,
For the second day of the Sabbath.

GREAT IS the Lord, and greatly to be praised in the city of our God, in his holy mountain,
2 In the whole earth's well-rooted joy. On Mount Zion, on the north side, in the city of the great King,
3 God is known in her towers whenever he brings help to her.
4 Behold, the kings of the earth assembled, they came on together,
5 They saw her so and they marveled, they were troubled, they were shaken,
6 Trembling seized hold of them, pangs as of a woman giving birth.
7 Thou shalt break up the ships of Tarshish with a violent wind.
8 As we have heard, so we have seen in the city of the Lord of hosts; in the city of our God, God has established her forever.   *Selah*
9 We have thought, O God, of thy mercy in the midst of thy temple.
10 According to thy name, O God, so is thy praise to the ends of the earth; thy right hand is full of righteousness.
11 Let Mount Zion be glad, let the daughters of Judah rejoice because of thy judgments, O Lord.
12 Encircle Zion and embrace her, tell her story in her towers,
13 Set your hearts on her strength and mark well her towers, that you may tell her story to the next generation.
14 For he is our God, forever our God, unto ages of ages; he will guide us for ages of ages.

PSALM 48
For the end of the struggle,
a Psalmic Ode concerning the Sons of Korah.

Hear this, all peoples, give ear, all inhabitants of the world, 2 Both low and high, rich and poor together.
3 My mouth shall speak wisdom; the meditation of my heart shall speak understanding.
4 I will incline my ear to a parable, I will open my dark saying on the harp.
5 Why should I fear in an evil day? The iniquity at my heels surrounds me.
6 Those who believe in their own power, those who boast of their vast wealth,
7 A brother could not redeem: no one could. For no one could give God a ransom even for himself—
8 Not the price of his own soul's redemption,
9 Though he labored for ages and ages and lived to the end of them.
10 And he shall not behold corruption when he sees wise men die, when the fool and the witless perish and leave their wealth to others,
11 And their graves will be their homes into all eternity, their dwelling places for all generations, though they called their lands after their own names.
12 A man in being honored has never understood that he has become like the mindless beasts.
13 Their road is their own stumbling block, and afterwards they will delight in the words of their own mouth.   *Selah*
14 Like sheep, they are laid in Hades, death shall be their shepherd; the upright shall rule them in the morning, their help shall wax old in Hades far away from their glory.
15 Yet God will redeem my soul from the hand of Hades when he shall receive me.   *Selah*
16 Do not be afraid when one becomes rich, when the glory of his house is increased,
17 For when he dies he shall carry nothing away, his glory shall not descend after him.
18 For his soul shall be blessed in his own lifetime; he will acknowledge thee when thou doest him good.

19 He shall enter the generations of his fathers, for all eternity he shall never see light.
20 A man in being honored has never understood that he has become like the mindless beasts.

Glory. Both now. Alleluia.

PSALM 49
A psalm of Asaph.

The God of gods, the Lord, has spoken, he has summoned the earth from the sun's rising to its very setting.
2 From Zion, his beauty's splendor, God will visibly come—
3 Our God—and shall not keep silence. A fire shall blaze before him, a mighty tempest surround him.
4 He shall summon heaven above and earth to judge his people.
5 Gather together to him his holy ones who established his covenant by sacrifices.
6 The heavens shall declare his righteousness, for God is judge. *Selah*
7 Hear, O my people, I will speak to thee, O Israel, I will affirm to thee: I am God, thy God,
8 I will not censure thee for thy sacrifices, nay, thy whole burnt offerings are continually before me.
9 I will not take a bull from thy house, nor goats out of thy folds.
10 For every beast of the forest is mine, the cattle in the hills and the oxen.
11 I know all the birds of the heaven, and the field's splendor is mine.
12 If I were hungry, I would not tell thee, for the world is mine and all its fullness.
13 Will I eat the flesh of bulls, or drink the blood of goats?
14 Offer to God a sacrifice of praise and pay to the Most High thy vows.
15 Call upon me in the day of thine affliction, and I will deliver thee, and thou shalt glorify me.   *Selah*
16 To the sinner God has said: Why dost thou declare my statutes, why dost thou take my covenant in thy mouth?
17 Thou hast hated instruction, casting my words behind thee.

18 If thou sawest a thief, thou didst run with him, keeping company with adulterers,
19 Giving thy mouth over to malice, thy tongue has woven deceits.
20 Thou didst sit and malign thine own brother; against thine own mother's son thou didst set up a stumbling block.
21 Thou hast done these things and I kept silent. Thou hast thought in thine evil that I was just like thee. But I will rebuke thee and reveal all this to thy face.
22 Understand this, you that forget God, lest he snatch you away and there be none to deliver:
23 A sacrifice of praise shall glorify me, that is the way I will show him the salvation of God.

PSALM 50
A psalm of David,
when Nathan the prophet came to him,
after he had gone in to Bathsheba, the wife of Uriah.

HAVE MERCY ON me, O God, according to thy great mercy; according to the abundance of thy compassion blot out my transgression.
2 Wash me thoroughly from my iniquity and cleanse me from my sin.
3 For I know my iniquity and my sin is always before me:
4 Against thee, thee alone, have I sinned; I have done evil before thee: that thou mayest be justified in thy words and victorious when thou art judged.
5 Behold, I was conceived in iniquities, in sins did my mother bear me.
6 Behold, thou hast loved the truth, thou hast made manifest to me wisdom's hidden and secret things.
7 Thou shalt sprinkle me with hyssop and I will be made clean, thou shalt wash me and I will be made whiter than snow.
8 Thou shalt make me hear joy and gladness, my humbled bones shall rejoice.
9 Turn thy face from my sins and blot out all my iniquities.
10 Create in me a pure heart, O God, and renew a right Spirit within me.

11 Do not cast me away from thy presence, do not take thy Holy Spirit from me.
12 Restore to me the joy of thy salvation and uphold me by thy guiding Spirit.
13 I will teach transgressors thy ways and the godless shall turn back to thee.
14 Deliver me from bloodguiltiness, O God, the God of my salvation, and my tongue shall rejoice in thy righteousness.
15 O Lord, thou shalt open my lips and my mouth shall declare thy praise.
16 For if thou hadst desired a sacrifice I would have given it; thou wilt not be pleased even with whole burnt sacrifices.
17 A sacrifice to God is a broken spirit, a broken and humbled heart God will not count as nothing.
18 Do good in thy good pleasure to Zion, and may Jerusalem's walls be built up.
19 Then thou shalt be pleased with a sacrifice of righteousness, with offering and whole burnt sacrifices; then shall they offer young bulls on thine altar.

Glory. Both now. Alleluia.

PSALM 51

For the end of the struggle, concerning instruction by David, when Doeg the Edomite had come to tell Saul that David had gone to the house of Abimilech.

WHY DOST THOU boast in evil, O mighty man, and in wickedness all the day long?
2 Thy tongue has devised unrighteousness, like a sharp razor thou hast worked treachery.
3 Thou hast loved evil more than good, wickedness more than speaking righteousness.   *Selah*
4 Thou hast loved all devouring words, thou hast loved a deceitful tongue.
5 Thus shall God utterly unmake thee, he shall pluck thee out of thy dwelling place, uproot thee from the land of the living.   *Selah*
6 The righteous also shall see and fear and shall laugh at him, saying:

7 This man did not make God his helper but trusted in the abundance of his riches, growing ever stronger in vanity.
8 But I am like a fruitful olive tree in the house of God, I have hoped in God's mercy unto ages of ages.
9 I will give praise to thee forever for what thou hast done, and I will wait on thy name, for it is good in the sight of thy saints.

PSALM 52
*For the end of the struggle,
a psalm of instruction by David upon the harp.*

THE FOOL SAID in his heart: There is no God. They are corrupt and abominable in wickedness, there is none who does good.
2 God looked from heaven on the sons of men to see if any understand or seek God.
3 They have all turned aside, altogether corrupted; there is none, not even one, who does good.
4 Do all the workers of wickedness know nothing at all? They eat up my people as they eat bread, and do not call upon God.
5 They were in great fear where no fear was, for God has scattered the bones of man-pleasers; they have been put to shame, for God has made them be nothing.
6 Who will give out of Zion the salvation of Israel? When God brings back the captivity of his people, let Jacob rejoice, let Israel be glad.

PSALM 53
*For the end of the struggle,
instruction by David when the Ziphites went to
Saul and said: Is not David hiding with us?*

SAVE ME, O God, in thy name and in thy power judge me.
2 O God, hear my prayer, give ear to the words of my mouth.
3 For strangers rose up against me, the powerful sought after my soul; they have not set God before them.   *Selah*
4 For behold, God is my helper, the Lord is protector of my soul,
5 He will bring evil upon my enemies. Utterly destroy them in thy truth.

6 Willingly I will sacrifice to thee; I will give thanks to thy name, O Lord, for it is good.
7 Thou hast rescued me from all my afflictions and my eye has looked down upon all my enemies.

PSALM 54
For the end of the struggle, a hymn of instruction by David.

GIVE EAR, O God, to my prayer, do not disdain my supplication,
2 Attend to me and hear me. I was depressed in my prayer and troubled
3 By the enemy's voice, by the sinner's oppression, for they turned their iniquity upon me, in wrath they raged against me.
4 My heart was troubled within me, the terror of death has fallen on me.
5 Fear and trembling have come upon me, the darkness has covered me.
6 I said: Who will give me wings like a dove, that I may fly away and be at rest?
7 See how far away I have fled, I have dwelt in the wilderness. *Selah*
8 I was awaiting my savior from faintheartedness and tempest.
9 Drown them in the depths, O Lord, and confuse their tongues, for I have seen iniquity and strife in the city.
10 Day and night it shall surround her, even to her walls, iniquity and toil and unrighteousness are in her midst
11 And usury and deceit have not departed from her streets.
12 For if an enemy had reviled me I would have borne it, if one hating me had bragged against me I would have hidden from him.
13 But it was thou, a man my equal, my guide and my acquaintance,
14 Thou that made sweet the meals we shared; in God's house we walked in one mind.
15 Let death come upon them, let them go down alive into hell, for wickedness is in their dwellings, in the very midst of them.
16 As for me, I have cried out to God and the Lord has heard me.
17 Evening and morning and midday I shall tell and proclaim of it, and he shall hear my voice.

18 He will redeem my soul in peace from those closing round me, for in many ways they have pressed me.
19 God will hear and humble them, he who exists before all the ages, *Selah*, for there is no ransom for them, because they have not feared God.
20 He has stretched forth his hand in retribution, they have defiled his covenant.
21 They were scattered by the wrath of his countenance, yet his heart drew near; their words were smoother than oil, yet they were drawn swords.
22 Cast your cares on the Lord and he shall sustain you, he will never permit the righteous to be shaken.
23 But thou, O God, wilt bring them down into the pit of destruction; bloodthirsty and deceitful men shall not live even half their days. As for me, O Lord, I shall hope on thee.

Glory. Both now. Alleluia.

KATHISMA EIGHT

PSALM 55
*For the end of the struggle,
a pillar inscription by David
when the Philistines took him in Gath, concerning
peoples separated from the holy things.*

HAVE MERCY ON ME, O LORD, for man has trodden me down; all day long he has afflicted me in war.
2　All day my enemies have trodden me down, for many war against me from on high.
3　By day I will not fear, I will put my hope in thee.
4　To God I will commend my words, on God I have set my hope, I will not be afraid what flesh can do to me.

5   All day long they made loathsome my words, all their thoughts were against me for evil.
6   They will dwell near, hiding themselves, they will dog my every step, as if lying in wait for my life.
7   On no account wilt thou save them, O God, in wrath thou wilt shatter whole peoples.
8   I have declared my life to thee, I have put my tears before thee.
9   Even as in thy promise my enemies shall be turned back in the day when I call upon thee; behold, I know thou art my God.
10 In God I will praise his command, in the Lord I will praise his word,
11 On God I have set my hope, I will not be afraid what man can do to me.
12 In me, O God, are vows of praise that I will render to thee,
13 For thou hast saved my soul from death, my feet from sliding, my eyes from tears, that I may be well-pleasing before God in the light of the living.

PSALM 56

For the end of the struggle; Do Not Destroy;
a pillar inscription by David, when he
fled Saul's presence into the cave.

HAVE MERCY ON ME, O God, have mercy, for my soul trusts always in thee; and in the shadow of thy wings I will hope until iniquity shall pass away.
2   I will cry out to God Most High, my God who is my benefactor.
3   He has sent out from heaven and saved me, he gave over to reproach those trampling me down. *Selah* God has sent out his mercy and his truth
4   And delivered my soul from young lions. I lay down like one troubled, amid sons of men, their teeth spears and arrows, their tongue a sharp sword.
5   Be exalted, O God, above the heavens; let thy glory be above all the earth.
6   They have set a snare for my steps, they bowed down my soul, they dug a pit right before me but fell into it themselves.   *Selah*

7 My heart is ready, O God, my heart is ready, I will sing and give praise in my glory.
8 Awake, my glory; awake, lute and harp! I will arise at daybreak.
9 I will praise thee, O Lord, among the peoples, I will sing to thee among the nations.
10 For thy mercy is magnified to the heavens, thy truth even to the clouds.
11 Be exalted, O God, above the heavens, let thy glory be above all the earth.

PSALM 57
*For the end of the struggle; Do Not Destroy;
a pillar inscription by David.*

Do you truly speak righteousness, do you judge rightly, O you sons of men?
2 For in your heart you work iniquities, your hands weave unrighteousness on earth.
3 Sinners are estranged from the womb, from birth they have erred, speaking lies.
4 Their rage is like a serpent's rage, like a deaf snake that stops its ears,
5 Not heeding the voice of enchanters, not spellbound by a wizard's spell.
6 God shattered their teeth in their mouths, the Lord broke the great teeth of the lions.
7 They will vanish like waters flowing by, he will bend his bow until they are weakened.
8 Like melting wax they will be destroyed, fire fell on them, they never saw the sun.
9 Before the bramble produces your thorns, while you are still alive, he will utterly unmake you.
10 The righteous man shall gladly rejoice when he beholds the vengeance, he shall bathe his hands in the blood of the sinners.
11 A man will say: If there truly is a reward for the righteous, then surely God judges those on earth.

Glory. Both now. Alleluia.

PSALM 58
For the end of the struggle; Do Not Destroy;
a pillar inscription by David, when Saul sent men
to watch his house and kill him.

RESCUE FROM my enemies, O God, redeem me from those rising up against me.

2 Deliver me from the workers of iniquity and save me from bloodthirsty men.

3 For behold they hunted down my soul, the mighty have set upon me, not for my iniquity, O Lord, nor my sin.

4 Without iniquity I ran straight on: Rise up and meet me, and behold!

5 And thou, O Lord God of hosts, the God of Israel, awake! Visit all nations of the earth, be merciless to all that work iniquity. *Selah*

6 They shall return each evening hungry like dogs circling a city.

7 Behold, they shall speak with their mouths and with swords on their lips, saying: Who has heard?

8 But thou, O Lord, shalt laugh at them, thou wilt hold all nations in contempt.

9 O my strength, I shall keep watch for thee, for thou art my helper, O my God.

10 My God, his mercy shall outrun me, God will make it known to me even amidst my enemies.

11 Do not slay them lest they forget thy law; scatter them by thy power, bring them down, O Lord my shield,

12 Bring down the sin of their mouth, bring down the words of their lips, let them be taken in their pride, and the end of all their lies and cursing

13 Will be proclaimed in a wrath of destruction, and they will be no more. And they shall know that God rules Jacob to the very ends of the earth.   *Selah*

14 They shall return each evening hungry, like dogs circling a city.

15 They shall be scattered to search for food, if they are not satisfied they grumble.

16 But I will sing of thy power, proclaiming thy mercy each morning, for thou hast become my helper, my refuge in the day of my affliction.

17 O my helper, I will sing to thee, for thou, O God, art my protector, my God and my mercy.

PSALM 59

For the end of the struggle, a pillar inscription by David in alternating verses, for instruction, when he had burned Syrian Mesopotamia and Syrian Sobol, and when Joab had returned and defeated the twelve thousand in the Valley of Salt.

O GOD, THOU DROVEST us off, destroying us, thou wast enraged at us, then hadst mercy.
2 Thou hast made the earth quake, thou hast broken it; heal its fractures, for it has been shaken.
3 Thou hast shown thy people harsh things, thou hast made us drink down the wine of deep repentance.
4 Thou hast given a clear sign to those who fear thee, that they may flee from the line of the bows. *Selah*
5 That thy beloved be rescued, save with thy right hand and hear me.
6 God has spoken in his sanctuary: I will exalt and divide Sikima, I will measure out the vale of tabernacles.
7 Galaad is mine, and mine is Manasseh, Ephraim is the strength of my head, Judah is my king.
8 Moab is the cauldron of my hope, over Idumea I will extend my sway, foreign tribes were subjected to me.
9 Who will bring me into a fortified city? Who will lead me as far as Idumea?
10 Wilt not thou, O God, who didst drive us away? Wilt not thou, O God, go out with our armies?
11 O give us help from affliction, for human salvation is emptiness.
12 In God we will work wondrous things, he will utterly scorn those who afflict us.

PSALM 60

For the end of the struggle, A psalmic hymn of David.

HEAR MY SUPPLICATION, O God, attend to my prayer.
2 From the ends of the earth I have cried out to thee, my heart engulfed in depression, and thou didst lift me high on a rock.

3 Thou hast guided me, for thou hast become my hope, a tower of strength against the enemy's face.
4 I will abide in thy tabernacle forever, sheltered in the shelter of thy wings.   *Selah*
5 For thou, O God, hast heard my prayers, thou hast given a heritage to those who fear thy name.
6 Thou wilt add days to the king's days, as many years as the days of generations.
7 He shall abide before God forever. Who shall seek out his mercy and truth?
8 So I will sing praise to thy name forever, that I may daily perform my vows.

Glory. Both now. Alleluia.

PSALM 61
*For the end of the struggle,
a psalm of David concerning Jeduthun.*

SHALL NOT MY soul be submissive to God? For from him is my salvation.
2 For he only is my God and my savior, my helper, so I shall be shaken no more.
3 How long will you attack a man? All of you keep on murdering as if he were a leaning wall, a sagging fence.
4 They also planned to savage my honor, they ran swiftly with lies, they blessed with their mouth but they cursed inwardly.   *Selah*
5 My soul, be submissive only to God, for my endurance is from him.
6 For he only is my God and my savior, my helper, so I shall never be moved.
7 In God is my salvation and my glory, he is the God of my help, my hope is in God.
8 Hope in him, all you congregation of people, pour out your hearts before him, for God is our helper.   *Selah*
9 Empty indeed are the sons of men, liars are the sons of men; in the scales of wrongdoing they are altogether emptiness.

10 Put no hope in wrongdoing, do not hunger for robbery; if riches flow in, do not set your heart on them.
11 God spoke once and for all and I heard both these things:
12 That dominion is God's, and to thee, O Lord, belongs mercy, for thou wilt give back to every man according to his works.

PSALM 62
A psalm of David, when he was in the Idumean desert.

O GOD, MY GOD, at dawn I seek thee; my soul thirsted for thee, my flesh so many times has thirsted for thee in a trackless desert where no water is.
2 So in the sanctuary I have appeared before thee to see thy power and thy glory.
3 Because thy mercy is better than life, my lips shall sing praise to thee.
4 Thus I will bless thee in my life, I will lift up my hands in thy name.
5 As if with marrow and fatness, my soul was made full; and my mouth shall sing praise to thee with lips filled with rejoicing.
6 When I remembered thee on my bed at daybreak I meditated on thee.
7 For thou art become my helper, and in the shelter of thy wings I will be glad and rejoice.
8 My soul has cleaved to thee, thy right hand has upheld me.
9 But those who sought vainly my soul shall go into the lowest places of earth.
10 They shall be given the sword's edge, they shall be portion for foxes.
11 But the king shall rejoice in God, all who swear by him shall be praised, for the mouths of liars are stopped.

PSALM 63
For the end of the struggle, a psalm of David.

HEAR MY VOICE, O God, when I pray to thee, raise up my soul from fear of the enemy.
2 Thou hast sheltered me from the swarm of evildoers, from the horde of those working wickedness,

3   Who sharpen their tongues like swords, who strung their bows of bitter words
4   To cut down in secret the blameless man; suddenly they will shoot and never fear.
5   They made an evil thing strong in themselves, they spoke of hiding snares, saying: Who will see them?
6   They searched out iniquities, searching without even searching. A man of deep heart shall draw near them
7   And God shall be exalted. Their blows became like little children's stings,
8   Their tongues grown slack in them. All beholding them were troubled,
9   And every man was terrified and proclaimed the works of God, comprehending his deeds.
10 The righteous man shall rejoice in the Lord and shall set his hope in him and all the upright in heart shall glory.

Glory. Both now. Alleluia.

KATHISMA NINE

PSALM 64
For the end of the struggle, a psalmic ode of David when Jeremiah, Ezekiel, and the captive people were about to depart.

TO THEE IS DUE A SONG, O God, in Zion; to thee shall the vow be performed.

2 O hear my prayer, for to thee shall all flesh come.

3 The words of lawless men overpowered us, but thou wilt show mercy to all our transgressions.

4 Blessed is he whom thou hast chosen and taken to thee, for he shall dwell in thy courts. We shall be filled with the goodness of thy house; holy is thy temple, wondrous in righteousness.

5 Hear us, O God our savior, the hope of all the ends of the earth and of those on faraway seas,
6 Fashioning mountains in thy strength, girded round with power,
7 Confounding the depths of the seas and the sounds of their waves. The nations will be churned up,
8 And those living at the earth's edges shall be terrified at thy signs: Thou shalt delight in daybreak and sunset.
9 Thou hast visited earth and watered it, thou hast abundantly enriched it, the river of God is filled with rich waters, thou hast prepared them their food; for thus is thy preparation.
10 Water the furrows abundantly, make the crops grow richly; growing, they shall rejoice in the rains.
11 In blessings, thou wilt crown the year with thy generous mercy, and thy fields will be filled with abundance.
12 The desert fruits will be enriched, the hills will be girded with rejoicing.
13 The rams are clothed in thick fleece, the valley shall abound in wheat; they shall shout, they shall sing for joy.

PSALM 65

For the end of the struggle, a psalmic ode of resurrection.

MAKE A JOYFUL shout to God, all the earth,
2 Sing now to his name, give glory to his praises.
3 How terrifying are thy works! Through the greatness of thy power shall thine enemies submit themselves to thee.
4 Let all the earth worship thee, let all sing praise to thee, let them sing praise to thy name.   *Selah*
5 Come and see the works of God; he is more terrifying in his counsels than are the sons of men.
6 He turns the sea into dry land, they pass over the river on foot.
7 There will we rejoice in him, who in his power will rule over the ages; his eyes will observe the nations, that the rebellious not exalt themselves.   *Selah*
8 O bless our God, you peoples, make the voice of his praise to be heard,
9 Who has set my soul into life, who steadied my feet from falling.

10 For thou, O God, hast tested us, thou hast tried us by fire as silver is purified by fire.
11 Thou hast brought us into the net, laying affliction on our backs.
12 Thou hast caused men to ride over our heads, we went through fire and water; but thou didst lead us into a breathing place.
13 I will enter into thy house with whole burnt offerings, I will pay thee my vows,
14 Which my lips have uttered and my mouth has spoken when I was in affliction,
15 I will offer thee fatted sacrifices with incense and rams, I will offer oxen with goats.   *Selah*
16 Come and hear, all you who fear God, I will recount all the things he has done for my soul.
17 I cried to him with my mouth, I exalted him with my tongue.
18 If I regard iniquity in my heart, let not the Lord hear me.
19 Therefore God has heard me, attending to the voice of my supplication.
20 Blessed be God, who has not turned away my prayer, nor his mercy from me.

PSALM 66
For the end of the struggle, a psalmic hymn of David.

GOD BE MERCIFUL to us and bless us, and cause his face to shine upon us,   *Selah*
2 That thy way may be known on earth, thy salvation among all nations.
3 Let the peoples praise thee, O God, let all the peoples praise thee.
4 O let the nations be glad and sing for joy, for thou shalt judge the people righteously and govern the nations on earth.   *Selah*
5 Let the peoples praise thee, O God, let all the peoples praise thee.
6 The earth has yielded her fruits; God, our own God, has blessed us,
7 God has blessed us. Let all the ends of the earth be in fear of him.

Glory. Both now. Alleluia.

PSALM 67
For the end of the struggle, a psalmic ode of David.

L ET GOD ARISE, let his enemies be scattered, let those who hate him flee from before his face.

2 As smoke vanishes so let them vanish, as wax melts before the fire so let the wicked perish from before his face.

3 But let the righteous be glad, let them exult in the presence of God, let them be gladdened with delight.   *Selah*

4 Sing to God, sing to his name, make ready the way for him who rides upon the sunsets, and rejoice in his presence.

5 Let them be troubled from before his face, for he is father to the fatherless, he is defender of the widows. God is in his holy place.

6 God sets the solitary in families, in courage setting free the shackled, those who rebel against him, even those dwelling in tombs.

7 O God, when thou didst march out in the presence of thy people, passing through the desert,   *Selah*

8 The earth shook, the heavens poured rain, at the presence of the God of Sinai, at the presence of Israel's God.

9 Thou, O God, wilt send plentiful rain to thy wearied inheritance, and thou didst restore it.

10 Thy creatures are dwelling in it; in thy great goodness, O Lord, thou hast provided for the poor.

11 The Lord will give his word to those proclaiming the glad tidings with great power.

12 He is King of the hosts of the beloved, and he will divide the spoils for the beauty of the house.

13 Even should you fall asleep at your post, you will have the wings of a dove, all covered with silver, with feathers like yellow gold. *Selah*

14 When he who is above the heavens ordains kings over her, they shall become as white as the snow on Zalmon.

15 The mountain of God is sweet butter, a mountain of richly sweet butter.

16 Why do you ponder other sweet mountains? This is the mountain where God dwells; yes, the Lord desires to dwell here forever.

17 God's chariot is ten thousandfold, countless thousands abounding in number; the Lord of Sinai is among them, in his holy place.

18. Thou hast ascended on high, thou hast led captivity captive, thou hast received gifts in men, for thou shalt make thy home even among the unbelievers.
19. Blessed be the Lord from day to day, the God of our salvation who will greatly enrich us.   *Selah*
20. Our God is the God of salvation, and to the Lord, to the Lord are the paths out from death.
21. But God will crush his enemies' heads, the hairy scalp of those trespassers who go on and on in their transgressions.
22. The Lord said: I will return from Bashan, I will return from the sea's depths,
23. That your foot may be dipped in blood, your dog's tongue in your enemies' blood.
24. Thy ways have been seen, O God, the ways of my God and my King in his holy place.
25. The princes came first, singers followed after; in the midst of them came young maidens playing tambourines.
26. Bless God in the congregations, the Lord, from the fountains of Israel.
27. There is the younger Benjamin in rapture, the Judean princes are their rulers, the princes of Zebulun and Naphtali.
28. Give command, O God, to thy power, empower, O God, what thou hast wrought for us.
29. Because of thy temple at Jerusalem, kings will bring presents to thee.
30. Rebuke the wild beasts in the reeds, the herd of bulls amidst the heifers of the peoples, lest they oust those proved like silver: Scatter the nations that delight in war.
31. Ambassadors shall come out of Egypt, Ethiopia shall quickly come to stretch out her hand to God.
32. Sing to God, you kingdoms of the earth, O sing praises to the Lord.   *Selah*
33. Sing praises to him who rides the heaven of heavens down into the dayspring. Behold, he will give with his voice, a voice of great power.
34. Give glory to God, whose magnificence is over Israel, whose power is in the clouds.

35 God is wondrous in his saints; the God of Israel shall give power and strength to his people. Blessed be God.

Glory. Both now. Alleluia.

PSALM 68
*For the end of the struggle, in alternating verses,
a psalm of David.*

Save me, O God, for the waters have flooded into my soul.
2 I sank in the sea's mire where there is no place to stand; I came into the sea's depths where the storm overwhelmed me.
3 I am wearied by crying, my throat hoarse, my eyes have grown weak from hoping for my God.
4 Those hating me without cause are more than the hairs of my head, my enemies have grown strong in persecuting me unjustly, I have paid restoration for things I never stole.
5 O God, thou knowest my foolishness, and my sins are not hidden from thee.
6 O Lord, Lord of hosts, let not those who wait for thee be put to shame because of me; O God of Israel, let not those who seek after thee be confounded because of me.
7 For thy sake I bore reproach, shame has covered my face.
8 I have become a stranger to my brothers, an alien to my mother's sons.
9 For the zeal of thy house has eaten me up, the reproaches of those reproaching thee have fallen upon me.
10 I bent down my soul with fasting, and that became my reproach.
11 I also made sackcloth my garment, I became a byword to them.
12 Those sitting at the gate kept prattling against me, those gulping down wine made up songs about me.
13 But I, O Lord, I pray to thee, it is the time, O Lord, of thy good pleasure, in the abundance of thy mercies; in the truth of thy salvation, hear me.
14 Save me from the mud that I be not mired down; free me from those hating me, from the waters' depths.
15 Let not a tempest of water drown me, let not the deep swallow me up, let not the pit shut its mouth on me.

16 Hear me, O Lord, for thy mercy is good; and according to thine abundant compassion, look attentively on me.
17 Turn not thy face from thy child, for I am afflicted, hear me speedily.
18 Draw near to my soul and redeem it, deliver me because of my enemies.
19 For thou knowest my reproach and my shame and humiliation; before thee are all my tormentors.
20 It was reproach my soul anticipated, and heavy misery; I waited for a fellow mourner but no one came, for comforters but I found none.
21 They gave me gall for my food, they gave me vinegar for my drink.
22 Let their table become a snare for them, for a recompense and a stumbling block.
23 Let their eyes be darkened so that they cannot see, bend down their backs continually,
24 Pour out thine anger upon them, let the fury of thy wrath seize hold of them.
25 Let their dwelling place be desolate, let no one live in their tents.
26 For they hounded the one thou hadst struck down, they intensified the pain of my wounds.
27 Add iniquity to their iniquity, let them not enter into thy righteousness.
28 Let them be blotted out from the book of the living and not be written with the righteous.
29 I am poor and suffering, O God, and the salvation of thy face has taken hold of me.
30 I will praise God's name with a song, I will magnify him in praise.
31 This shall be more pleasing to the Lord than a calf with horns and hooves.
32 Let the poor behold this and be glad. Seek God and your soul shall live.
33 For the Lord has heard the poor, he does not despise his prisoners.
34 Let heaven and earth praise him, the seas and everything that moves in them.
35 For God shall save Zion; the cities of Judah shall be built, they shall dwell there and they shall inherit it.

36 His servants' seed shall possess it, those that love his name shall dwell in it.

PSALM 69
*For the end of the struggle, a psalm of David
in remembering that the Lord has saved me.*

O God, give heed to my help; O Lord, make haste to help me.
2 May those seeking my soul be ashamed and confounded, may those desiring my hurt be turned back and confused.
3 May they be turned back at once who jeer at my hurt: Well done!
4 May all those seeking thee rejoice and be glad in thee; may those loving thy salvation continually say: Let God be magnified.
5 But I am poor and needy, O my God, help me. Thou art my helper and deliverer, O Lord, do not delay.

Glory. Both now. Alleluia.

KATHISMA TEN

PSALM 70
*A psalm of David, concerning Jonadab's sons
and those first taken captive;
untitled among the Hebrews.*

IN THEE, O LORD, I HAVE HOPED, may I never be put to shame.

2 Deliver me in thy righteousness, rescue me, incline thine ear to me and save me.

3 Be the God of my protection, the stronghold of my salvation, for thou art my rock and my refuge.

4 O my God, rescue me from the sinner's hand, from his transgressing and cruel hands.

5 For thou art my endurance, O Lord, my hope, O Lord, from my youth.
6 By thee I have been upheld from birth, from my mother's womb thou hast been my shelter, my song shall be always of thee.
7 I have become as a wonder to many, but thou art my strong helper.
8 Let my mouth be filled with thy praise that I may sing of thy glory, sing thy magnificence all the day.
9 Do not cast me off in the time of old age; when my strength fails do not forsake me.
10 For my enemies spoke against me, those stalking my soul have conspired against me,
11 Saying: God has abandoned him, pursue and lay hold of him, for there is none to rescue him.
12 O God, stand not far off from me; my God, make haste for my help.
13 Let those slandering my soul be disgraced and vanish away, let those seeking my hurt be covered in shame and reproach.
14 But I will hope continually and will praise thee yet more and more.
15 My mouth shall proclaim thy righteousness, thy salvation all the day long, for I know nothing about the worldly business of men.
16 I shall enter into the Lord's power, I shall remember, O Lord, thy righteousness, thine only.
17 Thou hast taught me, O God, from my youth, and from then until now I will proclaim thy wonders.
18 Even to my old age and great years, O God, do not abandon me, until I proclaim thy strength to all the coming generations, thy power and thy righteousness.
19 O God, the magnificent things thou hast done for me reach even to the very heights—O God, who is like thee?
20 How great and severe the afflictions thou hast shown me, yet thou didst relent and quicken me; thou hast led me up from the great depths of earth.
21 Thou didst increase thy greatness over me, then thou didst turn and comfort me; thou hast led me up from the great depths of earth.
22 I shall sing thy truth, O God, in the vessel of a psalm, I shall sing praise with the harp, O Holy One of Israel.

23 My lips shall greatly rejoice when I sing praises to thee, and so shall my soul rejoice which thou hast redeemed.
24 My tongue shall study thy righteousness all the day long whenever those seeking my hurt are disgraced and confounded.

PSALM 71
For Solomon, a psalm of David.

GIVE THE KING, O God, thy judgment, thy righteousness to the king's son,
2 That he may judge thy people in righteousness and thy poor with judgment.
3 Let the mountains bring peace to thy people and the hills bring righteousness.
4 He shall judge the poor of the people, he shall serve the sons of the poor, he shall humble the false accuser,
5 And he shall continue as long as sun and moon continue, for generations of generations,
6 And he shall come down like rain on the fleece, like raindrops streaming to earth.
7 In his days, righteousness shall flourish, and the abundance of peace, until the moon be no more.
8 And he shall have dominion from sea to sea, from the river throughout all the inhabited earth.
9 The Ethiopians shall fall down before him, his enemies shall lick the dust.
10 The kings of Tarshish and the isles shall come bearing gifts, the kings of Arabia and Saba shall bring offerings.
11 All the kings of the earth shall fall down and worship him, all nations shall serve him.
12 For he rescued the needy from the oppressor's hand, the poor who had no helper.
13 He shall spare the poor and needy, he shall save the souls of the needy.
14 He shall redeem their souls from usury and injustice, precious shall be their name in his sight.
15 He shall live, and Arabian gold shall be given to him; they shall pray to him without ceasing, all the day long shall they bless him.

16 He shall be a support on the earth even to the mountain peaks, his fruit shall surpass Lebanon; those of his city shall flourish like grass from the earth.
17 Let his name be blessed forever, his name shall outlast the sun, all peoples shall be blessed in him, all the nations shall bless him.
18 Blessed be the Lord God, the God of Israel, who alone does wondrous things.
19 And blessed be the name of his glory for ever and ever, unto ages of ages, and all the earth shall be filled with his glory: amen and amen!

Glory. Both now. Alleluia.

PSALM 72
A psalm of Asaph, an ode against the Assyrian.

Truly God is good to Israel, to those that are upright in heart.
2 Yet my feet had almost stumbled, my steps had nearly slipped.
3 For I had come to envy the lawless when I beheld their sinful peace.
4 For death holds no rejections for them, its whip possesses no strength.
5 Other men's sufferings are never theirs, they are never scourged with others.
6 Their arrogance thus overpowers them, they have wrapped themselves up in their violent unholiness.
7 Their evil shall arise as fatness, for they have entered into the hungers of their hearts.
8 They thought and spoke in wickedness, they spoke evil loftily.
9 They have set their mouth against heaven, their tongue has walked through the earth.
10 Thus my people shall turn from this, days of fullness shall be found in them.
11 They said: How can God know? Is there knowledge in the Most High?
12 Behold, these are the ungodly, they always flourish and prosper, in every age they have had riches.

13 In vain have I kept my heart just, in vain have I washed my hands with those who are innocent.
14 For all day long I was scourged, my rejection lasting through the night.
15 I said: If I should describe all this, I would break covenant with this generation of thy sons.
16 And I sought to understand all this, but it was painful work for me—
17 Until I come into God's sanctuary and comprehend what their end is.
18 Thou hast set evils indeed on them for their crafty dealings, thou hast cast them down in their exaltation.
19 O they became in an instant desolate, they vanished, wasted in their wickedness.
20 As dreams are to one awake, so, O Lord, thou shalt in thy city turn their idols to nothing.
21 For my heart had been blazing, my mind had been seared,
22 And I had become nothing and I did not understand, I had become a beast before thee.
23 And I am continually with thee, thou hast held fast my right hand,
24 In thy counsel thou hast guided me, with glory thou hast received me.
25 For what is there in heaven, what did I desire on earth but thee?
26 My heart and my flesh failed, but the God of my heart is my inheritance forever.
27 For those keeping far from thee, behold, they shall perish, all those who go whoring from thee thou hast utterly destroyed.
28 As for me, it is good to cling to God, to put my hope in the Lord, that I may proclaim all thy praises in the gates of Zion's daughter.

PSALM 73
A psalm of Asaph, concerning instruction.

O GOD, WHY HAST thou cast us off forever? Why has thine anger raged against the sheep of thy pasture?
2 Remember thy congregation thou hadst gained in the beginning, the rod of thine inheritance which thou hast redeemed, this Mount Zion where thou hast dwelt.

The Psalms of David

3 Raise up thy hands completely against their arrogance, against everything the enemy has done in thy holy places.
4 Those hating thee have boasted in the very midst of thy feast, they set up their banners for signs and they understood nothing.
5 As if entering from on high, as if into a thicket of trees,
6 They cut down the main doors; with battle axes and hammers they have smashed it down.
7 They have burned down thy sanctuary, they have defiled the tabernacle of thy name to the ground.
8 They said in their hearts, all of them bound together: Come let us completely burn down all God's feasts on the earth.
9 We do not see our signs, there is no longer any prophet, he would no longer know us.
10 How long, O God, will the enemy reproach? Will the adversary assail thy name forever?
11 Why dost thou stay thy hand, thy right hand forever at thy breast?
12 For God is our King before the ages, working salvation in the midst of the earth.
13 Thou hast made the sea strong by thy power, thou hast broken the heads of the dragons upon the waters.
14 Thou hast crushed the dragon's head, giving him as food for the peoples of Ethiopia.
15 Thou hast riven fountains and torrents and dried up the river of Ethan.
16 The day is thine and thine is the night, thou hast perfected the light and the sun.
17 Thou hast made every beauty of earth, summer and winter hast thou shaped.
18 Remember all this thy creation. The enemy has reproached the Lord, mindless people have assailed thy name.
19 Do not give over to savage beasts the soul that confesses thee, do not forever forget the souls of thy needy ones.
20 Have regard, O God, for thy covenant, for the dark places of the earth are full of the houses of cruelty.
21 Let not the humbled and disgraced be turned away; the poor and needy shall praise thy name.
22 Arise, O God, judge thine own cause, remember how the mindless man reproaches thee all day long.

23 Do not forget the voice of thy suppliants; the arrogance of those hating thee rises against thee continually.

Glory. Both now. Alleluia.

PSALM 74

For the end of the struggle; Do Not Destroy; a psalmic ode of Asaph.

W E SHALL CONFESS thee, O God, we shall confess thee, we shall call upon thy name.
2 I shall proclaim all thy wonders when I seize hold of the time; I shall discern rightly.
3 The earth is dissolved and all its inhabitants; I had made firm its pillars.   *Selah*
4 I said to the transgressors: transgress no more. And to the sinners I said: Be not exalted,
5 Do not magnify yourselves, do not speak wickedness of God.
6 For magnificence comes neither from the sunrise nor the sunset nor from the desert mountains,
7 For God is the judge; this one he brings down low, that one he raises up.
8 For the cup in the Lord's hand is brimming with strong wine, he has tipped it side to side, but its dregs have not been drained: All earth's sinners shall drink them down.
9 As for me I shall exult forever, I shall sing to the God of Jacob.
10 All the horns of sinners I shall shatter, but the horns of the righteous shall be exalted.

PSALM 75

For the end of the struggle, a psalmic ode of Asaph against the Assyrian.

IN JUDAH GOD is known, his name is great in Israel.
  2 His place was made in peace, his dwelling place in Zion.
3 There he broke the bow's power, shield, sword and battle.   *Selah*
4 Thou shinest wondrously forth from the everlasting mountains.
5 The senseless in heart were confounded, all the rich men slept their sleep and found nothing in their hands.
6 At thy rebuke, O God of Jacob, soldiers mounted on horseback fell into a light slumber.

7 Thou, O thou, art fearsome; who shall withstand thee in thy chastising wrath?
8 From heaven thou madest thy judgment heard, the earth feared and was still
9 When God arose to judgment to save all the gentle on earth. *Selah*
10 The inmost thoughts of man shall give praise to thee, the remainder of man's mind shall keep feast to thee.
11 Pray and make your vows to the Lord our God, and all those round about him shall bring offerings
12 To him who is fearsome, to him who takes as tribute every princely spirit, to him who is fearsome to all kings of the earth.

PSALM 76
For the end of the struggle, a psalmic ode of Asaph concerning Jeduthun.

With my voice I cried out to God, with my voice to God, and he gave ear to me.
2 In the day of my affliction I sought out the Lord, my hands uplifted all the night, and I was never once distracted.
3 I remembered God and was gladdened, I complained and my spirit grew weak. *Selah*
4 I held my eyelids open through all the watches of the night; I was so troubled I could not speak.
5 I considered the days of old, I remembered the ages long past in my meditation.
6 By night I communed in my heart, my spirit made diligent search.
7 Will the Lord cast me off forever? Will he be favorable no more?
8 Will he cut off his mercy completely, from generation to generation?
9 Will God forget to be merciful? Or will he in his anger withhold his compassion? *Selah*
10 I said: Now I have begun to see; this is a change being wrought by the right hand of the Most High.
11 I remembered the works of the Lord, for I will recall thy wonders of old,
12 And I will meditate on all thy work, I will ponder upon thy doings.
13 Thy way, O God, is in the sanctuary; who is so great a God as our God?

14 Thou art the God who works wonders, thou hast made thy power known among all thy peoples.
15 Thou hast with thine arm redeemed thy people, the sons of Jacob and Joseph.   *Selah*
16 The waters saw thee, O God, the waters saw thee and were afraid; the depths were troubled, the rush of great waters.
17 The clouds gave forth voice, for thine arrows ran through them,
18 The voice of thy thunder was in the wheeling winds, thy lightnings lit up the world, the earth trembled and shook.
19 Thy way is in the sea, thy path in the great waters, thy footsteps shall not be known.
20 Thou hast led thy people like a flock by the hand of Moses and Aaron.

Glory. Both now. Alleluia.

KATHISMA ELEVEN

PSALM 77
An instruction of Asaph.

GIVE HEED, O MY PEOPLE, to my law, incline your ears to the words of my mouth.

2 I shall open my mouth in parables, I shall utter things hidden since the foundation of the world,

3 Things we have heard and known, things that our fathers taught us.

4 They hid nothing from their children in the next generation, proclaiming the praises of the Lord and his mighty deeds and the wondrous works he has done.

5 He raised up a testimony in Jacob, he appointed the law in Israel, and he commanded our fathers to declare all the law to their sons,
6 So that the next generation would know, those sons yet to be born, and they in turn would arise to proclaim to their sons,
7 That they might set their hope in God and never forget the works of God and always seek his commandments,
8 That they not become like their fathers, a generation, twisted and rebellious, that did not keep its heart straight, whose spirit was not steadfast with God.
9 The armed sons of Ephraim carrying bows turned back in the day of battle.
10 They did not guard God's covenant, they failed to walk in his law,
11 And they forgot his gracious works and his wonders that he had shown them,
12 The wonders he had accomplished in the sight of their fathers, in Egypt in the plain of Tanis.
13 He split asunder the sea and led them all through, the waters standing straight up as if held in wineskins.
14 In a cloud, he guided them by day, all night in the radiance of fire.
15 He split the rock in the wilderness, having them drink from great depth
16 And making streams run from the rocks, making streams flow down in rivers.
17 Yet they kept sinning against him, in the desert they kept on rebelling against the Most High.
18 In their hearts they kept testing God, demanding he feed all their hungers.
19 And they spoke against God, saying: Why cannot God prepare a table in the wilderness?
20 Since he could smite the rock and make waters pour down in torrents, can he not also give bread or set a table for his people?
21 Hearing this, the Lord was enraged, and fire was kindled in Jacob, anger arose against Israel,
22 Because they did not believe in God nor put their hope in his salvation.
23 Yet he had commanded the clouds above and opened the doors of heaven,

24 Raining down on them manna to eat, giving them the heavenly food:
25 Men ate the very bread of angels, he sent them food to the full.
26 He brought the south wind down from the heavens and led in by his power a wind from the southwest.
27 He rained flesh down on them like dust, winged birds like sands of the sea,
28 Letting them fall amid their camps, falling all around their tents.
29 So they ate and were well filled, for he gave them their own desire.
30 They were not deprived of their desire, but even while the food was in their mouths
31 God's wrath rose up against them and cut down the stoutest of them, shackling the chosen of Israel.
32 In all these ways they kept sinning, not believing in his wondrous works,
33 And so all their days ended in emptiness, all their years in fear.
34 When he slew them they sought him and repented and rose up early in their prayers to God.
35 They remembered that God is their helper, the Most High God their redeemer.
36 So they loved him with their mouths but were lying to him with their tongues,
37 For their hearts were not straight with him, they were unfaithful to his covenant.
38 But he is compassionate and will be gracious to their sins and will not destroy them, again and again forgoing his wrath, never kindling all his anger.
39 For he remembered they are flesh, a breath that passes and never returns.
40 How many times, how many times did they provoke him in the wilderness, did they grieve him in the desert?
41 They turned away and tempted God, they provoked the Holy One of Israel.
42 They did not remember his hand in that day he freed them from the hand of the oppressor,
43 How he wrought his signs in Egypt, his wonders in the plain of Tanis,

44 And turned their rivers and rainfall into blood they could not drink.
45 He sent them swarms of devouring flies and frogs that destroyed them.
46 He gave their crops over to blight, their labor to the locust.
47 He destroyed their vines with hail, their mulberry trees with frost.
48 He also gave their cattle to the hail, all their substance up to fire.
49 He cast on them his anger's rage, anger and rage and affliction, as angels of destruction among them.
50 He made a path for his anger, not sparing their souls from death, and giving into death their cattle.
51 He struck down all the first-born in Egypt, the first-fruits of their labor in the tabernacles of Ham.
52 And he led out his people like sheep, he guided them like a flock out into the wilderness,
53 And he shepherded them in hope so that they never knew fear, and the sea covered up their enemies.
54 He brought them to the mountain of his holiness, this mountain his right hand had acquired.
55 He drove away the nations from before their face, apportioning them land by lots, and he settled in their tents all the tribes of Israel.
56 They tested God the Most High and they provoked him, not guarding his testimonies.
57 Like their fathers they turned back and acted faithlessly, changing direction like twisted bows.
58 They stirred him to anger with their sacrificial high places, they moved him to jealousy with their graven idols.
59 God heard them and disdained them, he rejected Israel utterly,
60 And he forsook the tabernacle of Shiloh, his dwelling place and home amidst men.
61 He gave their strength into captivity, their beauty into the enemy's hand.
62 He gave his people over to the sword, disdaining his own inheritance.
63 The fire consumed their young men, their maidens were not even mourned.
64 Their priests fell by the sword, none ever wept for their widows.

65 Then the Lord awoke as from sleep, like a strong man besotted with wine,
66 And he drove his enemies out, giving them into lasting disgrace.
67 And he rejected the dwelling of Joseph, he chose against the tribe of Ephraim.
68 He chose the tribe of Judah, this Mount Zion that he loved.
69 And he built there his high holy place, like the very heavens above, he founded it forever on the earth.
70 He chose David for his servant and took him from the sheepfolds,
71 From tending ewes great with young, to shepherd Jacob his people and his inheritance Israel.
72 So he was shepherd to them in the integrity of his heart, he guided them with skillfulness of hand.

Glory. Both now. Alleluia.

PSALM 78
A psalm of Asaph.

The nations, O God, have violated thine inheritance, they have defiled thy holy temple, they have made Jerusalem into a gardener's hut.
2 They have made thy servants' bodies into food for birds of the sky, the flesh of thy saints for beasts of the earth.
3 They have made their blood flow throughout all Jerusalem, there was no one to bury them.
4 We have become our neighbors' reproach, a scorn and a mockery to all those around us.
5 How long, O Lord? Wilt thou be angry forever? Will thy jealousy burn like fire?
6 Pour down thy wrath on the nations that ignored thee, on the kingdoms that never called on thy holy name.
7 For they have devoured Jacob and made desolate his dwelling place.
8 Do not remember our sins of old, let thy mercy come now to us, we have been brought very low.
9 Help us, O God our savior, for the glory of thy name, and deliver us, O Lord, being gracious to our sins for thy name's sake,

10 Lest the nations say: Where is their God? Let there be known amidst the nations, before our very eyes, that there is vengeance for thy servants whose blood has been poured out.
11 Let the prisoners' groaning enter thee; in full accord with thy majestic arm, keep alive the sons of the slain.
12 Pay our neighbors back sevenfold into their bosom that contempt, O Lord, of theirs which they have given thee.
13 For we are thy people, we are the sheep of thy pasture, we shall forever give thee thanks; from generation to generation we shall show forth thy praise.

PSALM 79

For the end of the struggle, a psalmic testimony of Asaph against the Assyrian, in alternating verses.

GIVE HEED, O thou shepherd of Israel, who leadest Joseph like a flock, who dwellest amidst the cherubim; O shine forth
2 In Ephraim, Benjamin and Manasseh, and awaken in thy power to come to us and save us.
3 Restore us, O God, shine thy countenance on us, we shall be saved.
4 O Lord God of hosts, how long wilt thou be angry against the prayer of thy people?
5 Wilt thou feed us the bread of tears, wilt thou give us as drink tears in full measure?
6 Thou hast cast us into all our neighbors' arguments, our enemies rained contempt on us.
7 Restore us, O God, shine thy countenance on us, we shall be saved.   *Selah*
8 Thou didst bring forth a vine from Egypt and, casting out the nations, thou didst plant it.
9 Thou didst make a path before it for its roots to grip and spread, and the land was filled.
10 Its shade covered the mountains, its boughs shadowed God's cedars,
11 Its branches reached to the sea, its tendrils as far as the river.
12 Why hast thou broken the fences so that all who pass on the road pluck and gather it?

13 The boar from the forest ravaged it, the savage beasts have devoured it.
14 Return now, O God of hosts, look down from heaven and see, come see closely this vine
15 And restore what thy hand planted, make perfect the son of man whom thou madest strong for thyself.
16 The vine was burned down and uprooted, but they shall utterly perish at thy countenance's rebuke.
17 Let thy hand be upon the man of thy right hand, upon the son of man whom thou madest strong for thyself.
18 Then we will never turn away from thee, thou wilt make us be alive, we will call upon thy name.
19 Restore us, O Lord God of hosts, shine thy countenance on us; we shall be saved.

PSALM 80

*For the end of the struggle,
a psalmic ode of Asaph concerning the wine-presses.*

Rejoice in God our helper, shout for joy to Jacob's God,
2 Raise up a psalm, sound the drum, the sweet psaltery and the lute,
3 Sound the trumpet at the new moon, on this our brightest feast day,
4 For this is Israel's ordinance, the decree of Jacob's God.
5 He made this a testimony for Joseph in his going out from Egypt's land, where he heard a tongue he never knew.
6 He lifted burdens from his back, freed his hands from heavy baskets.
7 In affliction, you called out to me and I delivered you; I have answered you in the hidden place of thunder, I have tested you in the waters of contention.   *Selah*
8 Hear, O my people, and I will speak to you; I will bear you witness, O Israel.
9 If you will hearken to me, there will never be a new god in you, nor will you worship strange gods.
10 I am the Lord your God, I led you up out of Egypt's land; open wide your mouth, I will fill it.

11 But my people did not hear my voice, Israel would have none of me,
12 And I let them go out in the habits of their own hearts, to go in their own habits.
13 If my people had heard me, if Israel had walked in my ways,
14 I would have brought down their enemies, my hand heavy on their oppressors.
15 The Lord's enemies have lied to him, but their doom will be forever.
16 He has fed them with the finest of wheat, and with honey from the rock he has satisfied them.

Glory. Both now. Alleluia.

PSALM 81
A psalm of Asaph.

GOD HAS STOOD in the mighty assembly, and in their very midst he judged among the judges.
2 How long will you judge unjustly and favor persons who are wicked? *Selah*
3 Defend the poor and orphaned, be just to the oppressed and needy;
4 Rescue the poor and needy, deliver them from the sinner's hand.
5 Neither knowing nor comprehending, they have gone on in darkness; all earth's foundations will be shaken.
6 I said: You are gods, you are all sons of the Most High.
7 But you shall die as men die, you shall fall like any earthly prince.
8 Arise, O God, judge the earth, for thou shalt inherit all nations.

PSALM 82
A psalmic ode of Asaph.

O LORD GOD, WHO can be likened to thee? Be not silent nor peaceful, O God,
2 For behold, thine enemies have roared, those that hate thee have raised up their heads.
3 They darkly plotted against thy people, in malice of will conspiring against thy saints.

4 They said: Let us destroy them all so their nation will exist no more, Israel's very name forever erased.
5 For they plotted with singleness of mind, forming an alliance against thee:
6 The tents of Idumea and the Ishmaelites, Moab and the Hagarenes,
7 Gebal and Ammon and Amalek, the Tyrian people with foreign troops,
8 Even Assyria has joined with them, becoming the helper of Lot's sons. *Selah*
9 Deal with them as thou didst deal with Madiam, with Madiam at Sisara, with Jabin at the brook of Kison,
10 Who were slaughtered at En Dor, who became as dung on the earth.
11 Make their princes like Oreb and Zeb, make all their princes like Zebee and Salmana,
12 Who said: Let us seize for ourselves the high holy place of God.
13 O my God, turn them like a wheel, like chaff before the wind's face.
14 As fires burn down forests, as flames consume whole mountains,
15 So in thy storming shalt thou hunt them down, in thy rage shalt thou dismay them.
16 Fill their faces with shame, O Lord, and they shall seek after thy name.
17 May they be disgraced and dismayed unto ages of ages, may they be confounded and destroyed,
18 So that they may know that thy name is Lord, that thou alone art Most High over all the earth.

PSALM 83

For the end of the struggle,
a psalm to the sons of Korah concerning the wine-presses.

How beloved thy dwellings, O Lord of hosts.
2 My soul longs, even faints for the courts of the Lord, my heart and my flesh have rejoiced in the living God.
3 For the sparrow has found a home, the turtledove a nest for herself where she will lay her young—even thine altars, O Lord of hosts, my King and my God.

4 Blessed are those who dwell in thy house; they shall praise thee unto ages of ages.   *Selah*
5 Blessed is the man, O Lord, whose help comes from thee, whose heart has ascended
6 Into the high valley of weeping, into the place thou hast set; for the lawgiver shall bestow blessings.
7 They shall go from strength to strength, the God of gods shall be seen appearing in Zion.
8 O Lord God of hosts, hear my prayer, give ear, O God of Jacob! *Selah*
9 O God, our protector, behold: Look upon the face of thy Christ.
10 For one day in thy courts is better than a thousand elsewhere, I would rather be laid low in the house of my God than dwell in the tents of the wicked.
11 For the Lord loves mercy and truth, God will bestow grace and glory; the Lord will never deny good things to those who walk in innocence.
12 O Lord of hosts, blessed is the man who sets his hope in thee.

PSALM 84

*For the end of the struggle,
a psalm to the sons of Korah.*

THOU HAST BEEN gracious, O Lord, to thy land, thou hast brought back the captivity of Jacob.
2 Thou didst forgive thy people their iniquity, thou hast covered all their sin.   *Selah*
3 Thou hast ended all thy wrath, thou hast turned from thy burning rage.
4 Restore us, O God of our salvation, and end thine anger against us.
5 Couldst thou really be angry forever, prolonging thine anger from generation to generation?
6 Having restored us, O God, thou wilt make us live again, thy people will rejoice in thee.
7 Show us thy mercy, O Lord, and grant us thy salvation.
8 I will hear what the Lord God will speak in me, for he will speak peace to his people and to his saints, to those turning their hearts to him.

9 His salvation is very close at hand to all those that fear him, that glory may dwell in our land.
10 Mercy and truth have met together, righteousness and peace have kissed each other.
11 Truth has arisen from the earth, righteousness has descended from heaven.
12 For the Lord shall give his good kindness, our land shall yield up its fruit.
13 Righteousness shall go before him and shall make his footsteps our pathway.

Glory. Both now. Alleluia.

KATHISMA TWELVE

PSALM 85
A prayer of David.

BOW DOWN THINE EAR, O Lord, hear me, for I am poor and needy.

2 Guard my soul, for I am holy; save thy servant, O my God, whose every hope is in thee.

3 Have mercy on me, O Lord, for all the day long I shall cry out to thee.

4 Gladden thy servant's soul, O Lord, for I have lifted my soul to thee.

5 For thou, O Lord, art gentle and good, rich in great mercy to all who call upon thee.

6 Give ear, O Lord, to my prayer, heed the voice of my supplication.
7 In the day of my affliction I cried out to thee, for thou hast answered me.
8 There are no other gods, O Lord, that can be likened to thee, no works like thy works.
9 All the nations thou hast shaped, O Lord, shall come and worship before thee, they shall glorify thy name,
10 For thou art great in working wonders, thou alone art a great God.
11 Lead me, O Lord, in thy way, I will walk in thy truth; and gladden my heart in the awe of thy name.
12 I shall confess thee, O Lord my God, in fullness of heart; forever I shall glorify thy name,
13 For great is thy mercy to me; thou hast brought my soul up from deepest Hades.
14 Transgressors have risen against me, O God, a violent mob sought after my soul, they have not set thee before them.
15 But thou, O Lord God, art gracious, longsuffering and compassionate, great in thy mercy and truth.
16 Look upon me and have mercy, give thy strength to thy child, save the son of thy handmaid.
17 Work in me a sign for good and let them that hate me now see it and be disgraced, for thou, O Lord, hast helped me and comforted me.

PSALM 86

A psalmic ode to the sons of Korah.

His foundations are on the holy mountains.
2 The Lord loves the gates of Zion more than all the dwellings of Jacob.
3 Glorious things, O city of God, have been spoken of thee.   *Selah*
4 I will remember Rahab and Babylon as those who know me, and behold also the Philistines of Tyre and the Ethiopian people: All these were born of her.
5 A man will call Zion his mother, a man truly born of her, for the Most High has himself laid the foundations of her.
6 The Lord shall fully describe in the writings of the peoples how these princes were born of her.   *Selah*
7 How joyous are all those who have their dwelling in thee.

PSALM 87

*A psalmic ode to the sons of Korah for the end of
the struggle, to be sung responsively on the harp,
concerning instruction to Ethan the Israelite.*

O Lord, God of my salvation, I have cried out day and night before thee.

2 Let my prayer come before thee; incline thine ear, O Lord, to my supplication.

3 For my soul was filled with troubles and my life drew close to Hades.

4 I am counted among those who go down into the pit, like a man no one would help, like a man free among the dead,

5 Like mangled men lying in graves whom thou rememberest no more, like those snatched from thy hand.

6 They have laid me in the lowest pit, in dark places, in death's shadow.

7 Thy wrath leaned heavy on me, thy waves all crashed down on me. *Selah*

8 My friends thou hast taken from me, I was made loathsome to them; betrayed, I could not escape.

9 My eye weakened with great poverty, O Lord, all day I cried out to thee, to thee I stretched out my hands.

10 Wilt thou work miracles for the dead? Can physicians really resurrect them to proclaim thy praises to thee? *Selah*

11 Shall anyone in the grave give an account of thy mercy? Or thy truthfulness in a ruined place?

12 Shall thy wonders be known in the dark? Thy righteousness in oblivion's land?

13 But I, O Lord, I cried out to thee, and in the morning my prayer shall draw very near to thee.

14 Why, O Lord, dost thou cast away my soul? Why turnest thou thy face from me?

15 I am poor and troubled since childhood; briefly raised up, I was brought down into the depths of bewilderment.

16 Thy furies have swept through me, thy terrors have utterly unmade me,

17 Swirling around me daily like waters, surrounding me from every side.
18 Thou hast taken loved ones and friends far from me, even anyone who knew me, because of my misery.

Glory. Both now. Alleluia.

PSALM 88

Instruction to Ethan the Israelite.

O Lord I will sing thy mercies forever, with my mouth I will proclaim thy truth from generation to generation.
2 For thou didst say: Mercy shall be fashioned forever; thy truth shall be established in the heavens.
3 I have made a covenant with my chosen, I have sworn to my servant David:
4 I shall preserve eternally thy seed; from generation to generation I shall directly fashion thy throne.   *Selah*
5 The heavens shall confess thy wonders and thy truth, O Lord, in the assembly of the saints.
6 Who in the heavens shall equal the Lord? Who among the sons of God shall be likened to the Lord?
7 Glorified in the counsel of saints, God is vast and fearsome to all those around him.
8 O Lord God of hosts, who is like thee? Thou art mighty, O Lord, and thy truth surrounds thee.
9 Thou rulest over the sea's strength, stilling the surging of the sea.
10 Thou hast laid low the arrogant man as if he were wounded; with the arm of thy might thou hast scattered thine enemies.
11 Thine are the heavens, thine the earth, thou hast founded the world and all the world's fullness.
12 Thou hast created the north and the sea, Tabor and Hermon shall exult in thy name.
13 Thine is the sovereign arm, let thy hand be strengthened, thy right hand be uplifted.
14 Righteousness and judgment are the foundations of thy throne, mercy and truth shall go before thy face.

15 Blessed the people who know the joyful sound, they shall walk, O Lord, in the light of thy countenance,
16 And they shall exult all day long in thy name, and in thy righteousness shall they be exalted.
17 For thou art their power's glory, in thy good pleasure our horn shall be exalted.
18 For from the Lord is our defense, from the Holy One of Israel, our King.
19 In that time thou didst speak to thy sons a prophetic vision, saying: I have bestowed help upon one who is mighty, raising up one chosen from my people.
20 I have found my servant David, with my holy oil I have anointed him,
21 For my hand shall sustain him, my arm shall strengthen him.
22 No enemy shall reap profit from him, the son of iniquity no longer shall do any evil to him.
23 I will cut his enemies to pieces right before his eyes, and I shall put to flight all those that hate him.
24 My truth and my mercy are with him, in my name shall his horn be exalted.
25 I will place his hand upon the sea, his right hand upon the rivers.
26 He shall cry to me, saying: Thou art my God and my father, the one who helps my salvation.
27 I shall make him my firstborn, higher than all earthly kings.
28 I shall keep my mercy always for him, forever faithful to my covenant with him.
29 I shall make his line last forever, his throne long as the days of heaven.
30 If his sons should abandon my law and not walk in my judgments,
31 If they should profane my statutes and not preserve my commandments,
32 I shall visit their transgressions with a rod, their sins with the lashing of whips.
33 But never, never shall I scatter all my mercy away from him; my truth I shall never betray,
34 My covenant I shall never profane, I shall never set aside the words gone out from my lips.

35 Once for all I swore by my holiness I would never play David false:
36 His line shall endure forever, his throne as the sun before me,
37 Forever fashioned as the moon to be faithful witness in heaven. *Selah*
38 Thou hast cast away and made nothing, thou hast rejected thy Christ.
39 Thou brokest covenant with thy servant, profaning his sanctuary to the ground.
40 Thou didst smash through all his defenses, setting terror in his stronghold.
41 All passersby have plundered him, his neighbors hold him in contempt.
42 Exalting his enemies' right hand, thou didst delight all his adversaries.
43 Deflecting his sword's aid, thou didst let him down in battle.
44 Thou didst keep the cleansing rites from him and cast his throne to the ground.
45 Thou hast shortened his allotted days, raining disgrace down upon him.   *Selah*
46 How long, O Lord; wilt thou turn away forever? Will thine anger always rage like fire?
47 Remember how I am created; didst thou fashion all men to no purpose?
48 Can any living man keep away death? Can any deliver his own soul from the hand of Hades?   *Selah*
49 Where, O Lord, are thy mercies of old that in thy truth thou sworest to David?
50 Remember the contempt, O Lord, I suffered in my heart, contempt all thy servants suffer from all the nations,
51 Contempt, O Lord, thine enemies have used to darken that reconciling exchange given by thy Christ.
52 Blessed be the Lord forever. Amen and amen.

Glory. Both now. Alleluia.

PSALM 89
A prayer of Moses, Man of God.

O Lord, thou hast been our refuge, from generation to generation.
2. Before the mountains came to be, before creation was fashioned, before the lands of our homes were, from everlasting to everlasting, thou, O God, art.
3. Let not man be debased and laid low; say: Return, O you sons of men.
4. For a thousand years in thy sight are like yesterday when it is past, and like a watch in the night.
5. Their years shall be as worthless things, their morning fading like young grass,
6. At dawn blooming, then fading, at dusk drooping all the way down, withered now and dried out.
7. For we were unmade by thy rage and rocked by thy wrath.
8. Thou hast set our iniquities before thee, our life in the light of thy countenance.
9. For all our days have faded away, in thy rage we have been unmade, our years having no more strength than a spider's web.
10. Our days may reach seventy years, and if we stay strong, perhaps eighty, but most of them are toil and sorrow; for when mildness comes upon us, we shall be chastened at last.
11. Who could measure thine anger's strength? In our awe, how measure thy wrath?
12. So make known thy right hand to us that our hearts be held fast in wisdom.
13. How long, O Lord? Relent! To thy servants be comforter.
14. We were filled by thy mercy every morning, all our days we rejoiced and were glad.
15. Gladden us for all the days thou didst humble us, for the years we saw only evil.
16. Behold thy servants and thy works, give guidance to their sons,
17. And let our Lord's splendor be upon us; guide the works of our hands rightly for us, the works of our hands guide aright.

PSALM 90
An ode of praise by David, untitled among the Hebrews.

He that lives in the help of the Most High shall abide in the shelter of Heaven's God,

2 And shall say: Thou art my helper and refuge, O, my God; I put all my hope in him,

3 He shall free me from hunters' snares, from every terrifying word.

4 His shoulders shall bend down over thee, under his wings shalt thou have hope, his truth a shield surrounding thee.

5 Thou shalt not fear the night's terror nor the arrow that flies by day,

6 Nor the thing moving in the darkness nor the midday demon of catastrophe.

7 A thousand shall fall at thy side, ten thousand at thy right hand, but it shall not come near thee.

8 But with thine eyes shalt thou comprehend, and see the rewards of sinners.

9 For thou, O Lord, art my hope. Thou hast made the Most High thy refuge.

10 No evils shall come close to thee, nor any scourge draw near thy home,

11 For he shall put his angels over thee, to guard thee on all thy ways.

12 In their hands they shall bear thee up, lest thou dash thy foot against a stone.

13 Thou shalt tread upon asp and basilisk, thou shalt trample the lion and the dragon.

14 Because he has set his hope in me, I will deliver him; and I will shelter him, because he has come to know my name.

15 He shall call out to me and I shall hear, in affliction I am with him, I shall lift him up and glorify him,

16 With length of days I will satisfy him, I will show him my salvation.

Glory. Both now. Alleluia.

KATHISMA THIRTEEN

PSALM 91
A psalmic ode for the Sabbath day.

HOW GOOD TO GIVE PRAISE to the Lord, to sing psalms to thy name, O Most High,
2 To proclaim every morning thy mercy and thy truth every night
3 On the harp of ten strings, with a joyful song on the lyre.
4 For thou hast made me glad, O Lord; in the world of thy creation will I rejoice, in the works of thy hands.
5 O Lord, how magnificent are thy works, how deep thy thought.
6 This shall the fool never know nor the senseless man comprehend:

7   Though the wicked rise up like the grass, though all the workers of iniquity look loftily down, it is they that may well be destroyed unto the ages of ages.
8   But thou, Lord, art the Most High for ages.
9   For behold, thine enemies, O Lord; for behold, thine enemies shall perish, all the workers of iniquity shall be scattered.
10 But my horn shall be exalted like the horn of the unicorn, my old age shall be blessed with the richest compassion.
11 My eye has beheld my enemies, my ear shall grow keen in hearing of those workers of evil that keep rising against me.
12 The righteous shall flourish like a palm tree, he shall grow like the cedar in Lebanon.
13 Those taking deep root in God's house shall flourish in the courts of our God,
14 Still bearing fruit in a rich old age, living on in a splendor of being
15 That proclaims my Lord is upright, that he has no unrighteousness in him.

PSALM 92
*For the Sabbath vigil, an ode of praise by David,
when the earth was first peopled.*

THE LORD IS King, he is robed in majesty; the Lord is robed in strength and has girded himself, for he has established our lands so that they shall never be shaken.
2   From of old is thy throne prepared, from all eternity, thou art.
3   The rivers, O Lord, have lifted up, the rivers have uplifted their voices, the rivers shall raise their strong floods with the voices of many waves.
4   Wondrous is the surging of the sea, wondrous is the Lord on high.
5   Thy testimonies were steadfastly made, holiness befits thy house, O Lord, unto length of days.

PSALM 93
A psalm of David, for the fourth day of the week.

THE LORD GOD of vengeances, the God of vengeances, has openly declared himself.
2   Rise up, O judge of the earth, give the arrogant their reward.

Kathisma Thirteen

3 How long, O Lord, will sinners, how long will sinners arrogantly speak,
4 Uttering and repeating wickedness—all these workers of iniquity, how long shall they speak?
5 They brought down thy people, O Lord, they have wrecked thine inheritance,
6 They have killed immigrant and widow, they have murdered the orphaned,
7 Saying: The Lord will never see, the God of Jacob will never understand.
8 Understand, O senseless of the people, O fools, comprehend at last!
9 He who planted the ear, shall he not hear? He who formed the eye, shall he not see?
10 He who disciplines all nations, who guides all men to knowledge, shall he not rebuke?
11 The Lord knows the reasonings of man, that they are emptiness.
12 Blessed is the man, O Lord, whom thou shalt chastise, teaching him out of thy law
13 And making evil days cease for him until a pit be dug for the wicked.
14 For the Lord will not cast off his people, nor will he forsake his inheritance,
15 Until righteousness shall once more enter into all judgment, all the upright in heart possessing it.   *Selah*
16 Who will rise up for me against sinners, or side with me against evildoers?
17 If the Lord had not helped me, my soul would swiftly have gone down into Hades.
18 If I said that my foot slipped, thy mercy, O Lord, upheld me.
19 In the swarm of my heart's agonies, thy comforting, O Lord, has delighted my soul.
20 Shalt thou really be present on a throne of iniquity that frames evils by law?
21 They shall hunt the righteous man's soul and shall condemn innocent blood.
22 But the Lord has become my refuge, my God the helper of my hope,

23 And he shall bring down on them their very own iniquity, and in accord with their wickedness shall the Lord our God blot them out utterly.

Glory. Both now. Alleluia.

PSALM 94
An ode of praise by David, untitled among the Hebrews.

Come, let us rejoice in the Lord, let us shout in joy to God our savior,
2 Let us come gratefully before his face, let us raise joyful psalms to him.
3 For the Lord is a great God, a great King over all the gods.
4 In his hand are the earth's farthest places, the mountain heights are his also.
5 The sea is his, for he created it, his hands fashioned the dry land.
6 Come, let us worship and fall down before him, let us weep before the Lord our creator.
7 For he is our God and we are his pasture's people, the sheep of his hand.
8 Today, if you hear his voice sound, do not harden your hearts, as on the day of temptation when you rebelled in the wilderness,
9 When your fathers tested me and put me on trial, even though seeing my works.
10 I was grieved forty years with that generation, and I said: Their hearts always go very wrong, they have never known my ways.
11 And so I swore in my wrath they should never enter my rest.

PSALM 95
An ode of praise by David,
when the house was rebuilt after the captivity;
untitled among the Hebrews.

O sing to the Lord a new song; sing to the Lord, all the earth.
2 Sing to the Lord, bless his name, proclaim from day to day his joyous salvation.
3 Declare his glory among the nations, his wonders among all peoples.

4   For the Lord is great and he is greatly to be praised, and to be feared above all other gods.
5   For all the gods of the nations are demons, but the Lord made the heavens.
6   Graceful praise and splendor are in his presence, holiness and majesty in his sanctuary.
7   Bring to the Lord, O families of nations, bring to the Lord glory and honor,
8   Bring to the Lord the glory due his name, come bearing sacrifices into his courts,
9   Worship the Lord in his holy court, let all the earth be shaken before him.
10 Say among the nations: The Lord is King, he has established the earth so that it shall never be shaken, he shall judge the peoples righteously.
11 Let the heavens rejoice, let the earth exult, let the sea in all its fullness be shaken.
12 Then the fields and everything in them shall be filled with joy, all the trees and forests shall exult
13 Before the Lord's countenance, for he is coming, he is coming to judge the earth; he shall judge all the lands in righteousness, all the peoples with his truth.

PSALM 96
David's, when his land is restored;
untitled among the Hebrews.

The Lord is King, let the earth exult, let the countless islands be glad.
2   Clouds and darkness surround him, righteousness and judgment established rightly his throne.
3   Fire shall go out before him, burning his enemies on every side.
4   His lightnings lit up the lands, the earth saw and was shaken.
5   The mountains melted like wax in the Lord's presence, in the presence of the Lord of all earth.
6   The heavens proclaimed his righteousness, all the peoples beheld his glory.

The Psalms of David

7 Let them be disgraced, all who worship the carved images, all who boast of their idols: Worship him, all you his angels.
8 Zion heard and exulted; the daughters of Judah rejoiced because of thy judgments, O God.
9 For thou art the Lord Most High over all the earth, exalted most greatly over all the gods.
10 You who love the Lord, hate evil. The Lord guards the souls of his saints and shall deliver them out from the hands of the wicked.
11 Light has dawned for the righteous, gladness for the upright in heart.
12 Rejoice, O you righteous, in the Lord, singing praises and giving thanks for the remembrance of his holiness.

Glory. Both now. Alleluia.

PSALM 97
A psalm of David.

Sing a new song to the Lord, for he has worked wondrous things; with his right hand and holy arm he has won victory.
2 The Lord has made known his salvation, his righteousness he has revealed in the sight of the nations.
3 He has remembered his mercy to Jacob and his truth to Israel's house: His salvation has been seen to the very ends of the earth.
4 Shout joyfully to God, all the earth, sing and exult in sounding psalms,
5 Sing psalms to the Lord on a lyre, on a lyre and in psalmic voice,
6 Like trumpet call and blare of horn, sing joyfully to the Lord our King.
7 Let the sea in all its fullness tremble, the lands and all those dwelling there.
8 The rivers shall clap their hands, the mountains shall exult together in the presence of the Lord,
9 For he comes to judge the earth, he shall judge the lands with righteousness and the peoples with equity.

Kathisma Thirteen

PSALM 98
A psalm of David.

The Lord is King, let the peoples be enraged. He rests upon the cherubim, let the earth be shaken.
2 The Lord is great in Zion, he is exalted above all peoples.
3 Let them sing thanks to thy great name, for it is fearsome and most holy.
4 The King's honor loves fair judgment; thou hast established equity, bringing forth in Jacob fair judgment and righteousness.
5 Exalt the Lord our God, worship at the footstool of his feet, for he is holy.
6 Moses and Aaron are among his priests, and Samuel also is among those who call upon his name, they called upon the Lord, and he answered them,
7 He spoke to them in a pillar of cloud, for they kept his testimonies and the ordinances he gave them.
8 Thou, O Lord our God, didst answer them, again and again, O God, forgiving them, while rightly avenging all their misdeeds.
9 Exalt the Lord our God and worship at his holy mountain, for the Lord our God is holy.

PSALM 99
A psalm of David for a thank-offering.

Shout joyfully to God, all the earth,
2 Serve the Lord with gladness, come into his presence with joyous song.
3 Know that the Lord, he is God, that he has made us, and not we ourselves, that we are his people and the sheep of his pasture.
4 Enter into his gates with thanksgiving, and into his courts with praise, be thankful to him and bless his name.
5 For the Lord is good, his mercy is everlasting, and his truth endures to all generations.

PSALM 100
A Psalm of David.

To thee, O Lord, will I sing of mercy and judgment,
2 I will chant with wisdom in a perfect way. When wilt thou come to me? I have walked within my house with a perfect heart.
3 I have not set before my eyes any works of transgression, I have hated evildoers.
4 A twisted heart never clung to me; the evil man who shunned me, I never knew him.
5 The one who secretly slanders his neighbor, I kept turning away from him; the one with arrogant look and ravenous heart, I would never break bread with him.
6 I kept my gaze fixed upon the faithful in the land; the one walking on the perfect way, he would serve God with me.
7 No worker of evil would ever dwell in the midst of my house, no speaker of wicked things would ever stand straight in my eyes.
8 I kept on every morning slaying all the sinners on the earth, so as to uproot from God's city all those who work iniquity.

Glory. Both now. Alleluia.

KATHISMA FOURTEEN

PSALM 101
*A prayer of a poor man,
when he is depressed and pours
out his supplication before the Lord.*

HEAR MY PRAYER, O LORD, and let my cry come to thee.
2 Do not turn thy countenance from me; in the day I am afflicted, incline thine ear to me; in the day I call out to thee, hear me speedily.
3 For my days have vanished like smoke, my bones consumed like wood in a fire.

The Psalms of David

4. I have been cut down like the grass, and my heart has become so withered I have forgotten to eat my bread.
5. Because of the sound of my groaning, my bones have clung to my flesh.
6. I have become like a desert pelican; like an owl perched in the ruins,
7. I kept watch and have now become like a sparrow alone on a housetop.
8. My enemies reproached me all day long; even those who once praised me kept swearing falsely against me.
9. For I kept eating ashes like bread, kept mingling my drink with weeping,
10. Because of thy countenance's furious wrath, for thou didst lift me up, then throw me down.
11. My days are a lengthening shadow, I have withered away like the grass.
12. But thou, O Lord, shalt forever endure; thy memory is from generation to generation.
13. Arising, thou shalt have compassion on Zion, for the time of mercy for her has come, the right moment has come.
14. For thy servants took pleasure in her stones, they shall have compassion even for her dust.
15. So the nations shall fear thy name, O Lord, all the kings of the earth thy glory.
16. For the Lord shall build up Zion, he shall appear in his glory.
17. He has regarded well all humble prayer, he has not despised their pleas.
18. Let this prayer in psalm be written down for the generation to come, that the people yet to be created may give praise to the Lord.
19. For he looked down from his high holy place, the Lord looked from heaven to earth
20. To attend to the prisoners' groaning, to set free the sons of the slain,
21. To declare the Lord's name in Zion, and his praise in Jerusalem,
22. When the peoples are gathered together, and the kingdoms, to serve the Lord.

23 From his strength's path, he said to him: Tell me the fewness of my days,
24 Take me not away, O my God, in the midst of my days; thy years are throughout all generations.
25 In the beginning, O Lord, thou didst found the earth; the heavens are the works of thy hands.
26 They will perish but thou shalt endure; all things will wear out like a garment, and like a cloak thou shalt change them, and they shall be changed.
27 But thou art the same, and thy years shall never fail.
28 Thy servants' sons forever shall dwell, their seed guided rightly forever.

PSALM 102
David's.

BLESS THE LORD, O my soul; all that is within me, bless his holy name.
2 Bless the Lord, O my soul, and forget not all he has given,
3 Who forgives all thine iniquities, who heals all thy diseases,
4 Who redeems thy life from corruption, who crowns thee with mercy and compassion,
5 Who satisfies thy desire with good things, and thy youth is renewed like the eagle's.
6 The Lord performs great works of mercy and justice for all the oppressed.
7 He made known his ways to Moses, and his will to Israel's sons.
8 The Lord is merciful and gracious, slow to anger and abounding in mercy.
9 He will never be fully enraged, nor will he keep his anger forever.
10 He did not deal our sins back to us, nor give us what our evils deserved.
11 As far as heaven extends over earth, so the Lord has made his mercy extend over those who fear him.
12 As far as the east stands from the west, so far has he taken our sins from us.
13 As a father has compassion for sons, so will the Lord have compassion upon those who fear him,

14 For he well knows our fashioning, he has remembered that we are dust.
15 As for man, his days are like grass; as a flower of the field so he flourishes.
16 Then the wind has passed over and he shall be gone, he shall no longer know the place.
17 But the Lord's mercy is for all eternity upon all those who fear him, and his righteousness upon sons of sons,
18 To such as shall keep his covenant and remember to do his commandments.
19 The Lord prepared his throne in heaven, his kingship is supreme over all.
20 Bless the Lord, all you his angels, mighty in strength to do his word, in hearing the sound of his words.
21 Bless the Lord, all you his hosts, his ministers that obey his will.
22 Bless the Lord, all his works, in all places of his dominion. Bless the Lord, O my soul.

Glory. Both now. Alleluia.

PSALM 103
David's, on the creation of the world.

Bless the Lord, O my soul. O Lord my God, how magnificently dost thou exist, clothed in thanksgiving and majesty,
2 Arrayed in light as with a garment, stretching out the heavens like a curtain.
3 He covers his high halls with the waters, appointing the clouds for his staircase, ascending on the wings of the wind,
4 Making his angels his spirits, his ministers a flame of fire.
5 He established earth on her sure foundations, she shall never give way unto ages of ages.
6 The deep like a garment is his clothing, the waters shall stand upon the mountains.
7 At thy rebuke they shall flee, at the crash of thy thunder, they shall tremble with fear.
8 The mountains rise up, the valleys sink down, to the place thou hast founded for them.

9 Thou didst set a boundary never to be passed, the waters shall never again cover the earth.
10 Sending the springs into the valleys, he shall make the waters flow between the mountains.
11 They shall give water to every beast, the wild asses shall quench their thirst.
12 The birds of heaven shall dwell by them, from amidst the rocks they shall sing forth.
13 He waters the mountains from his upper chambers. The earth shall be satisfied with the fruit of thy works.
14 Growing the grass for the cattle, raising green plants to serve man, he brings forth bread from the earth
15 And wine to gladden man's heart, oil to make bright his face and bread to strengthen his heart.
16 The trees of the plain shall be fed, the cedars of Lebanon that thou didst plant.
17 In them shall the sparrows make nests, the heron's home greatest among them.
18 On the high hills are the deer, the cliffs are a refuge for the hyrax.
19 He made the moon to mark seasons, the sun knows the time to set.
20 Thou makest darkness and it is night when all the forest beasts will prowl,
21 The young lions roaring for their prey, seeking their food from God.
22 When the sun rises, they will gather and lie down in their dens.
23 Man shall go out to his work and shall labor until the evening.
24 O Lord, how manifold are thy works, in wisdom thou hast made them all. The earth is filled with thy creations,
25 As is this great and spacious sea that teems with countless things, living things both small and great.
26 There the ships ply their way, there is that Leviathan that thou madest to play there.
27 All of them look to thee alone to give them food in due season.
28 When thou givest they shall gather in, when thou openest thy hands everything shall be filled with goodness.

29 But when thou turnest thy face away they shall be deeply troubled, when thou takest their breath away they shall die back again to dust.
30 Thou shalt send forth thy Spirit and they shall be created, thou shalt renew the face of the earth.
31 May the Lord's glory endure forever; the Lord shall be glad in his works.
32 He gazes on the earth and it trembles, he touches mountains and they smoke.
33 I will sing to the Lord all my life, I will sing psalms to my God for as long as I have being.
34 May my thoughts be pleasing to him, and I shall be very glad in the Lord.
35 May the sinners vanish from the earth, may the wicked wholly cease to be. Bless the Lord, O my soul.

Glory. Both now. Alleluia.

PSALM 104
Alleluia.

O GIVE THANKS TO the Lord, call upon his name; make known his deeds among the peoples.
2 Sing to him, sing psalms to him, recount all his wondrous works.
3 Be praised in his holy name, let the hearts of those rejoice who are seeking the Lord.
4 Seek the Lord and be strengthened, seek his countenance continually.
5 Remember the wonders he has wrought, his marvels, and the judgments of his mouth,
6 O seed of Abraham his servant, you sons of Jacob, his chosen ones.
7 He is the Lord our God, his judgments are in all the earth.
8 He remembered his covenant forever, the word that he commanded for a thousand generations,
9 The word he spoke to Abraham, the oath he swore to Isaac,
10 The ordinance he gave to Jacob as Israel's everlasting covenant,
11 Saying: I shall give you Canaan as the land that you inherit.

12 When they were very few in number and scattered as strangers in the land,
13 Wandering from nation to nation, from one kingdom to the next,
14 He allowed no man to wrong them, reproving even kings on their behalf:
15 Never touch my anointed people, never do my prophets wrong.
16 He called down famine on the land, he sheltered all their sustenance.
17 He sent on a man before them, Joseph sold into slavery.
18 They shackled his feet with fetters, his soul passed into the iron
19 Until his prophetic word came true, the teaching of the Lord testing him with fire.
20 The king sent and released him, the ruler of the people set him free.
21 He made him lord of his house, ruler over all his possessions,
22 To instruct his princes in his name and to teach his elders wisdom.
23 Israel also came into Egypt, Jacob sojourning in the land of Ham.
24 He increased his people greatly, making them stronger than their enemies,
25 Whose hearts he turned to hate his people, to deal craftily with his servants.
26 He sent Moses his servant, and Aaron whom he had chosen.
27 He set among them the words of his signs, his wonders in the land of Ham.
28 He sent darkness and made it dark, and they rebelled against his words.
29 He turned their waters into blood and he destroyed their fish.
30 Their land abounded with frogs, even in the chambers of their kings.
31 He spoke and the dog-fly came, gnats swarmed within all their borders.
32 He sent them hail for rain, fire swept through all their land.
33 He smote their vines and their fig trees, he broke every tree in their lands.
34 He spoke, and there came locusts, swarms of locusts beyond number,
35 And they devoured all their grasslands, they devoured every fruit of the land.

36 And he smote the first-born in their land, all the first-fruits of their labor.
37 He led them out with silver and gold, not one man of their tribes growing weak.
38 Egypt rejoiced at their exodus, for fear of them had fallen upon them.
39 He spread a cloud as a cover for them, a fire to shine at night for them.
40 They asked, then the quails came, he filled them with the heavenly bread.
41 He split the rock and the waters flowed, the rivers ran in the waterless places.
42 For he remembered his holy word, he spoke to his servant Abraham.
43 He brought out his people with joy, his chosen ones with gladness,
44 And he gave them the lands of the nations, and they inherited the labors of peoples,
45 That they might keep his statutes, that they might seek after his law.

Glory. Both now. Alleluia.

KATHISMA FIFTEEN

PSALM 105
Alleluia.

O GIVE THANKS to the Lord, for he is good, for his mercy endures forever.
    2 Who shall speak the Lord's mighty acts? Who shall make all his praises be heard?
3 Blessed are they that keep his judgment, that practice righteousness at all times.
4 Remember us, O Lord, in thy good favor to thy people, visit us with thy salvation,

5 That we might behold the goodness of thy chosen, that we might be glad in the gladness of thy nations, that we might sing praise with thine inheritance.
6 We have sinned with our fathers, we have committed iniquity, we have done wickedly.
7 Our fathers while in Egypt did not understand thy wonders, did not remember thy vast mercy, but rebelled at the Red Sea.
8 Yet he saved them for his name's sake, that they might know his power.
9 When he rebuked the Red Sea, it dried up, and he led them through the deeps as he had led them through the desert.
10 He saved them from the hands of those who hated them, he plucked them out of hateful hands.
11 The waters covered their enemies, there was not one of them left.
12 Then they believed his words, and then they sang his praise.
13 But in hurrying they forgot his word, they no longer in patience awaited his counsel,
14 But in the wilderness they desired their desires, and in the waterless place they put God on trial.
15 And he gave them their request and sent fullness into their souls.
16 When they angered Moses in the camp and Aaron the saint of the Lord,
17 The earth opened up and swallowed Dathan and covered the assembly of Abiram.
18 A fire was kindled in their assembly, the flame burned up the sinners.
19 They made a calf in Horeb, and they worshiped the graven image.
20 Thus they exchanged his glory for an image of a calf eating grass.
21 They forgot God their savior, who had done great things in Egypt,
22 Wondrous works in the land of Ham, fearsome deeds by the Red Sea.
23 And he said he would have destroyed them had not Moses his chosen one stood before him in the breach to turn away his wrath lest he should destroy them.
24 Then they despised the desirable land; they did not believe his word,
25 But murmured in their tents, and they did not hear the Lord's voice.

26 So he raised his hand against them, to cast them down in the wilderness,
27 To cast down their seed among the nations, to scatter them over the lands.
28 They were initiated into Baal-Peor, they ate sacrifices of the dead.
29 They provoked him with their practices, destruction multiplied among them.
30 Then Phinehas stood to make atonement and at once the destruction ceased,
31 And it was reckoned as his righteousness by every generation for eternity.
32 They also greatly enraged him at the waters of contention, and Moses suffered for their sakes,
33 For they rebelled against his Spirit, so that he spoke judgment with his lips.
34 They did not destroy the nations as the Lord commanded them,
35 But mingled with the nations and took on all their ways,
36 And served their graven images that became a tempting snare for them,
37 And they sacrificed their sons and their daughters to the demons,
38 And they poured out innocent blood, their sons' and daughters' blood, in sacrifice to Canaan's idols, the land sick with murdered blood,
39 The land polluted with these deeds, but they kept whoring on and on in their ways and practices.
40 Enraged in fury against his people, the Lord abhorred his own inheritance,
41 And he gave them into enemy hands, and those who hated them were lords over them.
42 And their enemies afflicted them; they were humbled under their hands.
43 Over and over he rescued them, but they provoked him with their plotting and were brought low for their iniquity.
44 But he saw them in their agony when he heard their supplication,
45 And he remembered his covenant and repented in his great mercy.
46 And he aroused compassion for them from those who held them captive.

47 Save us, O Lord our God, gather us from among the nations, to give thanks to thy holy name and receive the glory of thy praise.
48 Blessed be the Lord God of Israel from everlasting to everlasting, and all the peoples shall say: Amen and amen.

Glory. Both now. Alleluia.

PSALM 106
Alleluia.

Give thanks to the Lord, for he is good, for his mercy endures forever.
2 So let them say, those that the Lord has redeemed, those he redeemed from the enemy's hands,
3 Assembled from out of all the lands, from the east and from the west, from the north and from the south.
4 They wandered in the waterless desert, they found no city to dwell in,
5 And in their hunger and thirst their life fainted in them.
6 In affliction they cried out to the Lord and he set them free from their anguish,
7 Guiding them on a straight path to a city they could dwell in.
8 Let them thank the Lord for his mercies, his wonders worked for the sons of men,
9 For he satisfied the empty soul, filling the hungry soul with good things:
10 Those sitting in the dark shadow of death, those shackled in poverty's chains
11 For rebelling against God's teachings and scorning the will of the Most High.
12 Their hearts were thus broken by labors, thus they grew weak and there was no one to help.
13 In affliction they cried out to the Lord and he saved them from their anguish,
14 He led them out of death's dark shadow, he broke their bonds asunder.
15 Let them thank the Lord for his mercies, his wonders worked for the sons of men,

16 For he shattered the gates of bronze, he crushed down the bars of iron.
17 He helped them out of their lawless way, for their iniquity had brought them down low.
18 Their soul abhorred all manner of food, they drew near to the gates of death.
19 In affliction they cried out to the Lord and he saved them from their anguish,
20 He sent his word and healed them, he delivered them from their corruption.
21 Let them thank the Lord for his mercies, his wonders worked for the sons of men,
22 Let them give him a sacrifice of praise, proclaiming his works with rejoicing.
23 Those who go down to the sea in ships, who do business on great waters,
24 They have seen the works of the Lord and his wonders in the deep.
25 He spoke and the stormwinds arose, their billows lifted on high,
26 Waves mounting up to the heavens, then crashing down to the depths: their souls consumed by these evils,
27 Shaken, they staggered like drunken men, all their wise skills swallowed up,
28 And in affliction they cried out to the Lord, and he led them out from their anguish.
29 At his command the winds became breezes, the raging billows fell into silence.
30 Then they rejoiced for their stillness, for his guiding them to his will's haven.
31 Let them thank the Lord for his mercies, his wonders worked for the sons of men,
32 Let them lift up a song to him in the assembly of the people, let them give praise to him in the council of the elders.
33 He turned the rivers into desert, the watersprings into parched ground,
34 A fruitful land into salt marsh, for the evil done by those living there.

35 He turned the desert into water pools, the parched ground into rushing streams,
36 There he made the hungry dwell, and they built cities to dwell in,
37 They sowed fields and planted vineyards that yielded abundant harvest.
38 He blessed them and they greatly multiplied, he never once decreased their herds.
39 But they were diminished and brought down by afflictions of evil and sorrow.
40 Scorn poured down from the princes, making them wander in a trackless waste where there was never a way.
41 Yet he helped the poor out from poverty, making their families like a flock.
42 The righteous shall see this and exult, all iniquity shall keep its mouth shut.
43 Who in wisdom shall keep these things? Who shall understand the mercies of the Lord?

Glory. Both now. Alleluia.

PSALM 107
A psalmic ode of David.

My heart is ready, O God, my heart is ready; I will sing and give praise in my glory.
2 Awake, lute and harp, I will arise at daybreak.
3 I will praise thee, O Lord, among the peoples, I will sing to thee among the nations.
4 For thy mercy is magnified to the heavens, thy truth even to the clouds.
5 Be exalted, O God, above the heavens, let thy glory be above all the earth.
6 That thy beloved ones be rescued, save with thy right hand, and hear me.
7 God has spoken in his sanctuary: I will exult and divide Sikima, I will measure out the vale of tabernacles.
8 Galaad is mine, and mine is Manasseh, Ephraim is the strength of my head, Judah is my king.

9 Moab is the cauldron of my hope, over Idumea I will extend my sway, foreign tribes were subject to me.
10 Who will bring me into a fortified city? Who will lead me as far as Idumea?
11 Wilt not thou, O God, who drove us away? Wilt not thou, O God, go out with our armies?
12 O give us help from affliction, for human salvation is emptiness.
13 In God we will work wondrous things; he will utterly scorn those who afflict us.

PSALM 108
For the end of the struggle, a psalm of David.

O GOD, DO NOT in silence pass over my praise.
2 For the mouth of the sinner and the mouth of the wicked have opened against me; they have spoken against me with a deceitful tongue,
3 They have surrounded me with words of hatred; for no cause they warred against me.
4 In return for my loving them they kept on accusing me falsely, but I kept on praying.
5 They repaid me evil for good and hatred for my love.
6 Set a wicked man over him, a satanic accuser at his right hand.
7 When on trial, let him be condemned, let his prayer become sin.
8 Let his days be very few, and let another take his office,
9 Let his sons become fatherless, let his wife become a widow,
10 Let his sons become homeless beggars cast out from ruined dwellings.
11 Let the creditor seize all that he has, strangers plundering his labors.
12 Let there be no one to help him, no one to have mercy on his orphans,
13 Let his children be utterly destroyed, in a single generation his name blotted out.
14 Let the Lord forever remember the sin of his fathers, let the sin of his mother never be blotted out.
15 Let them be continually before the Lord, let their memory perish from the earth

16 Since he never remembered to show mercy, since he persecuted the poor and needy, since he even sought to slay the heartbroken.
17 And as he loved cursing, so let it come to him; as he never wanted blessing, so let it be far from him.
18 He put cursing on like a garment; it has drenched him like water, seeping like oil into his bones.
19 Let it cover him like his clothing, let it gird him round like his belt.
20 Thus work my accusers before the Lord, those who speak against my soul.
21 But thou, O Lord, my Lord, deal with me in thy name's mercy, for thy mercy is greatly good.
22 Deliver me, I am poor and needy, my heart is troubled within me.
23 I have faded like a vanishing shadow, shaken off like some locust.
24 My knees have weakened from fasting, my flesh has failed from no oil.
25 And I have become their contempt, seeing me they shook their heads.
26 Help me, O Lord my God, in accord with thy mercy, save me,
27 Let them know that this is thy hand, that thou, O Lord, hast wrought this.
28 They will curse but thou shalt bless; let those be disgraced that rise up against me, but let thy servant rejoice.
29 Let my satanic accusers be clothed with humiliation, let them wrap themselves up in the mantle of disgrace.
30 I shall give abundant thanks to the Lord with my mouth, in the midst of great crowds I shall praise him greatly,
31 For he has stood closely by the right hand of the poor, to save me from those who are persecuting my soul.

Glory. Both now. Alleluia.

KATHISMA SIXTEEN

PSALM 109
A psalm of David.

THE LORD SAID to my Lord: sit at my right hand until I make thine enemies thy footstool.

2 The Lord shall send from Zion the scepter of thy power: Have dominion in thine enemies' midst.

3 With thee shall be dominion in the day of thy power, in the brightness of thy saints: From the womb before the morning star I have begotten thee.

4 The Lord has sworn and he will not repent: Thou art priest forever after the order of Melchizedek.

5 The Lord at thy right hand has completely broken kings in the day of his wrath.
6 He shall judge among the nations, filling them up with dead bodies, crushing the heads of many on earth.
7 He shall drink from the brook on the way, therefore he shall lift up his head.

PSALM 110
Alleluia.

I SHALL PRAISE THEE, O Lord, with my whole heart, in the council of the upright and in the congregation.
2 Great are the works of the Lord, discernible in all things that he has willed.
3 Gratitude and majesty are his work, his righteousness endures for all ages.
4 He has made a memorial of his works, the Lord is gracious and merciful.
5 He has nourished those who fear him, he will always remember his covenant.
6 He has unveiled to his people the power of his works in giving them to inherit the nations.
7 The works of his hands are truthfulness and judgment, faithful are all his commandments,
8 Established unto ages of ages, fashioned in truth and uprightness.
9 He sent redemption to his people, he commanded his covenant forever; holy and fearsome is his name.
10 The fear of the Lord is the beginning of wisdom, all those who practice this possess right discernment. His praise endures for all ages.

PSALM 111
Alleluia.

BLESSED IS THE MAN who fears the Lord, who in his commandments shall take great delight.
2 His seed shall be mighty on earth, the generation of the upright shall be greatly blessed.

3   His house has glory and wealth, his righteousness endures for all ages.
4   For the upright, he is the dawn light rising up in the darkness, merciful, compassionate and righteous.
5   A good man compassionately lends, he will guide his words with judgment,
6   For he shall remain forever unshaken; the righteous shall be in everlasting remembrance,
7   He shall not fear evil tidings, his heart readied to hope in the Lord.
8   In steadfast heart, he shall never fear and shall look straight at his enemies.
9   Giving, he has dispersed to the poor; righteousness is his for all ages, his horn shall be exalted with glory.
10 The sinner shall see this with rage, gnashing his teeth he shall melt away, the sinner's desire shall utterly perish.

Glory. Both now. Alleluia.

PSALM 112
Alleluia.

PRAISE THE LORD, O you his servants, praise the name of the Lord.
2   Blessed be the name of the Lord henceforth and forevermore.
3   From the sun's rising to its setting, praise the name of the Lord.
4   The Lord is high above all nations, his glory above the heavens.
5   Who is like the Lord our God, who dwells in the highest
6   And beholds the humble things in the heavens and upon the earth?
7   He lifts up the poor man from earth, he raises the needy up from dunghills,
8   To have him sit down with princes, with the very princes of his people.
9   He grants the barren woman a home, to be the joyful mother of children.

PSALM 113
Alleluia.

1. IN ISRAEL'S EXODUS from Egypt, Jacob's house from an alien people,
2. Judah became his sanctuary, and Israel his dominion.
3. The sea beheld this and fled, the Jordan river flowed backward,
4. The mountains skipped like rams, the hills like flocks of lambs.
5. O sea, what made thee flee? And turned thy flow, O Jordan?
6. Mountains, why did you skip like rams? You hills, like flocks of lambs?
7. The earth shook in the Lord's presence, in the presence of Jacob's God,
8. When he turned rock to standing pools, flint into fountains of waters.
9. Not unto us, O Lord, not unto us, but to thy name give glory, for thy mercy and thy truth's sake,
10. Lest the nations keep saying: Where, just where is their God?
11. Our God is in the heavens above, and both in heaven and on earth all things he willed he has done.
12. A nation's idols are silver and gold, the work of men's hands.
13. They have mouths but cannot speak, eyes they have but cannot see,
14. They have ears but cannot hear, noses they have but cannot smell,
15. They have hands but cannot touch, feet have they but cannot walk, their throats can make no sound.
16. Let their makers become like them, so let all who trust in them.
17. But Israel's house has hoped in the Lord, he is their help and their defender.
18. Aaron's house has hoped in the Lord, he is their help and their defender.
19. All those that fear the Lord have hoped in the Lord, he is their help and their defender.
20. The Lord has remembered us and helped us, he has blessed the house of Israel, he has blessed the house of Aaron,
21. He has blessed those fearing the Lord, even the least with the greatest.
22. May the Lord grant you increase, to you and to your sons.
23. You are blessed by the Lord who has fashioned heaven and earth.

24 The heaven of heavens is the Lord's, but he has given the earth to the sons of men.
25 The dead, O Lord, shall never praise thee, nor those who descend into Hades,
26 But we the living shall bless the Lord henceforth and forevermore.

PSALM 114
Alleluia.

I AM FILLED WITH love, for the Lord shall hearken to the voice of my supplication,
2 For he inclined his ear to me, and throughout all my days I shall call out to him.
3 The agonies of death surrounded me, the dangers of hell loomed over me, I found affliction and grief.
4 Then I called upon the Lord's name: O Lord, deliver my soul.
5 The Lord is merciful and righteous, and God has mercy on us.
6 The Lord is the guardian of infants, I was brought low and he saved me.
7 Return, O my soul, to thy peace, the Lord has been very good to thee,
8 He has delivered my soul from death, my eyes from tears, and my feet from faltering.
9 I shall be well-pleasing to the Lord in the land of the living.

Glory. Both now. Alleluia.

PSALM 115
Alleluia.

I BELIEVED AND THEREFORE I spoke: I was deeply cast down.
   2 I said in my terror: Every man is a liar.
3 What can I give back to the Lord for all he has given to me?
4 I will take up the cup of salvation and call upon the name of the Lord.
5 I shall pay my vows to the Lord in the presence of all his people.
6 Precious in the sight of the Lord is the death of his saints.
7 O Lord, I am thy servant, thy servant and thy handmaiden's son; thou hast broken apart my bonds,

8   I will sacrifice to thee a sacrifice of praise and call upon the Lord's name.
9   I shall pay my vows to the Lord in the presence of all his people,
10 In the courts of the Lord's house, in thy very midst, O Jerusalem.

PSALM 116
Alleluia.

PRAISE THE LORD, all you nations, sing praises to him, all peoples,
2   For immense is his mercy for us, the truth of the Lord forever endures.

PSALM 117
Alleluia.

GIVE THANKS TO the Lord, for he is good, for his mercy endures forever.
2   Let the house of Israel say he is good, for his mercy endures forever.
3   Let the house of Aaron say he is good, for his mercy endures forever.
4   Let all those who fear the Lord say he is good, for his mercy endures forever.
5   From amidst my affliction I called out to the Lord, and he heard me and led me forth into a large place.
6   The Lord is my helper, I shall never fear what someone could do to me.
7   The Lord is my helper, I shall see my enemies fallen.
8   Better to put trust in the Lord than to trust in men,
9   Better to set hope on the Lord than to hope in princes.
10 All the nations surrounded me, but in the name of the Lord I held them at bay,
11 They circled and circled me, but in the name of the Lord I held them at bay,
12 They circled me like bees at a nest, they blazed up like wildfire in dry grass, but in the name of the Lord I held them at bay.
13 Violently shoved, I was going to fall, but the Lord in an instant helped me.

14. The Lord is my strength and my song, he has become my salvation.
15. The joyous sound of salvation is in the tents of the righteous, the right hand of the Lord has worked mightily,
16. The Lord's right hand exalted me, the right hand of the Lord has worked mightily.
17. I shall not die, I shall live and proclaim the works of the Lord.
18. In chastising, the Lord disciplined me, but he did not give me to death.
19. Open to me the gates of righteousness, I shall enter, praising the Lord.
20. This is the gate of the Lord, here the righteous shall enter.
21. I shall give thanks to thee, for thou hast heard me, thou hast become my salvation.
22. The stone that the builders rejected has become the chief cornerstone,
23. And this has come from the Lord, and it is wonderful in our eyes.
24. This is the day the Lord has made, let us rejoice and be glad in it.
25. O Lord, O Lord, save us, help us, O Lord, abundantly.
26. Blessed is he who comes in the name of the Lord; we have blessed all of you from the house of the Lord.
27. God is the Lord and has appeared unto us; celebrate the feast with flourishing boughs, even to the horns of the altar.
28. Thou art my God, I shall give thanks to thee; thou art my God, I shall exalt thee, I shall give thanks to thee, for thou hast heard me and hast become my salvation.
29. Give thanks to the Lord, for he is good, for his mercy endures forever.

Glory. Both now. Alleluia.

KATHISMA SEVENTEEN

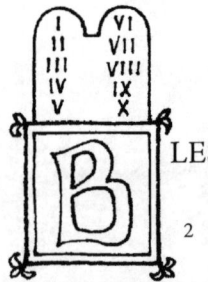

PSALM 118
Alleluia.

ALEPH

BLESSED ARE THE BLAMELESS in the way,
  Who walk in the law of the Lord.
2 Blessed be those searching his testimonies,
  Who seek him with the whole heart.
3 For the workers of iniquity
  Have never walked in his ways.
4 Thou hast charged that thy commandments
  Be kept most diligently.

5   O that my ways be all directed
To the keeping of thy statutes.
6   Then I shall not be ashamed
When I behold all thy commandments.
7   I shall praise thee with upright heart
As I learn thy righteous judgments.
8   I shall keep thy statutes,
Do not utterly forsake me.

BETH

9   How shall a young man make straight his way?
In the keeping of thy words.
10   I have sought thee with my whole heart,
Let me not stray from thy commandments.
11   In my heart I have hidden thy teachings,
That I might not sin against thee.
12   Blessed art thou, O Lord,
Teach me thy statutes.
13   With my lips I have declared
All the judgments of thy mouth.
14   I delight in the way of thy testimonies
As much as in every kind of wealth.
15   I shall deeply ponder thy commandments,
I shall comprehend thy ways.
16   I shall meditate in thy statutes,
I shall never forget thy words.

GIMEL

17   Give thy servant this reward:
That I shall live and keep thy words.
18   Take away the veil from my eyes
That I may see the wonders in thy law.
19   I am a stranger on the earth,
Hide not thy commandments from me.
20   My soul has always longed to desire
Thy judgments at every moment.
21   Thou didst rebuke the proudly arrogant,
Cursed be they that reject thy commandments.
22   Take from me reproach and contempt

For I have sought thy testimonies.
23 For princes sat and spoke against me,
But thy servant pondered on thy statutes.
24 Thy testimonies are my meditation,
Thy statutes my counselors.

DALETH

25 My soul lies prostrate on the earth,
Quicken me according to thy word.
26 I declared my ways, and thou didst hear me,
Teach me thy statutes.
27 Make me comprehend the way of thy statutes,
I shall ponder thy wondrous works.
28 My soul has fainted from depression,
Strengthen me with thy words.
29 Put the unjust way far from me,
With thy law have mercy on me.
30 I have chosen the way of truth,
I have never forgotten thy judgments.
31 I have clung to thy testimonies,
O Lord, put me not to shame.
32 I have run the way of thy commandments
When thou didst enlarge my heart.

HE

33 Give me as law, O Lord, the way of thy statutes,
And I shall seek it out always.
34 Give me wisdom to search deeply thy law,
I shall keep it with my whole heart.
35 Guide me on the path of thy commandments
For I have desired this.
36 Incline my heart to thy testimonies
And not to endless desirings.
37 Turn away my eyes from empty things,
Quicken me to live in thy way.
38 Establish thy teaching in thy servant
That I may be rooted in fear of thee.
39 Take away my scorn, which I dread,
For thy judgments are gracious.

40 Behold, I have longed for thy commandments,
   Quicken me in thy righteousness.

WAW

41 Let thy mercy, O Lord, come upon me,
   Thy salvation according to thy teaching.
42 I shall answer those who taunt me,
   For I have hoped on thy words.
43 Take not the word of truth
   Completely from my mouth
   For I have hoped in thy judgments.
44 So I shall keep forever thy law,
   Always and unto ages of ages.
45 I kept on walking in spaciousness,
   For I sought always thy commandments.
46 I kept on speaking of thy testimonies
   Even to kings, never once ashamed.
47 I kept on meditating in thy commandments
   For I have deeply loved them.
48 With upraised hands, I loved thy commandments,
   And I kept on pondering thy statutes.

ZAYIN

49 Remember thy word to thy servant
   By which thou hast given me hope.
50 This comforted me in my affliction
   For thy teaching has given me life.
51 The arrogant have greatly transgressed,
   But I have never swerved from thy law.
52 I remember thine eternal judgments, O Lord,
   I have been comforted.
53 Depression has seized me seeing the sinners
   Who everywhere abandon thy law.
54 Thy statutes have been my songs
   In the house of my pilgrimage.
55 In the night I remembered thy name,
   O Lord, and I kept thy law.
56 All this has happened to me
   Because I have searched deeply thy statutes.

HETH

57 Thou, O Lord, art my inheritance,
   I said I would keep thy word.
58 I pleaded before thy countenance
   With all my heart: Have mercy on me
   According to thy teaching.
59 I gave my reason over to thy ways,
   I turned my feet over to thy testimonies.
60 Untroubled, I have made myself ready
   In the keeping of thy commandments.
61 Sinners have ensnared me with cords,
   But I have never forgotten thy law.
62 At midnight I rose to give thee thanks
   For the righteousness of thy judgments.
63 I am companion of those fearing thee,
   Of those keeping thy commandments.
64 Thy mercy, O Lord, fills all the earth,
   Teach me thy statutes.

TETH

65 With grace thou hast dealt with thy servant,
   O Lord, according to thy word.
66 Teach me goodness, discipline and knowledge,
   For I have believed thy commandments.
67 Before I was humbled, I transgressed,
   Therefore I have kept thy teaching.
68 Thou art good, O Lord, and in thy goodness
   Teach me thy statutes.
69 The wickedness of the arrogant
   Has multiplied against me,
   But with my whole heart
   I shall search deeply thy commandments.
70 Their heart has gone sour like milk,
   But I have meditated in thy law.
71 It is good thou hast humbled me,
   That I might learn thy statutes.
72 The law of thy mouth is better to me
   Than thousands of gold and silver.

Glory. Both now. Alleluia.

YOD

Thy hands formed and fashioned me,
Teach me to know thy commandments.
74 Those fearing thee will rejoice seeing me
Because I have hoped in thy words.
75 I know, O Lord, thy judgments are righteous,
That with truth thou hast humbled me.
76 Let now thy mercy be for my comfort,
According to thy teaching to thy servant.
77 Let thy compassions rest upon me,
Then I shall live, for thy law is my meditation.
78 Let the proud be disgraced,
Who have transgressed against me unjustly,
But I shall meditate in thy commandments.
79 Let those fearing thee turn to me,
Those who know thy testimonies.
80 Let my heart be blameless in thy statutes,
That I may never be disgraced.

KAPH

81 My soul faints for thy salvation,
I have hoped in thy word.
82 My eyes dimmed in awaiting thy teaching,
Saying: When wilt thou comfort me?
83 I am shriveled like a wineskin in frost,
Yet I have never forgotten thy statutes.
84 How many are the days of thy servant?
When wilt thou judge my tormentors?
85 Transgressors have spread stories about me,
But they are far from thy law.
86 All thy commandments are truth,
Help me: I am unjustly persecuted.
87 They almost ended my life on earth,
But I never once forgot thy commandments.
88 Quicken me to live by thy mercy,
I shall keep the testimonies of thy mouth.

LAMED

89 Unto all eternity, O Lord,
   Thy word endures in heaven,
90 Thy truth unto generations of generations,
   Thou didst found the earth and it endures.
91 By thine ordering, each day endures,
   For all earthly things are thy servants.
92 If thy law had not been my meditation,
   I would have perished in my affliction.
93 I shall never forget thy statutes,
   In them thou hast quickened me to life.

midpoint*

94 I am thine, O Lord, save me,
   For I have sought thy statutes.
95 Sinners lurked for me to kill me,
   But I comprehended thy testimonies.
96 I have seen the limits of all achievements,
   But thy commandment is immensely spacious.

MEM

97 How I have loved, O Lord, thy law,
   It is my meditation all the day long.
98 Thou hast made me wise in thy commandment
   Above my enemies, and forever it is mine.
99 I comprehended more than all my teachers,
   For thy testimonies are my meditation.
100 I comprehended more than the elders,
    Because I sought always thy commandments.
101 I restrained my feet from every evil way
    That I might keep thy word.
102 I have never rejected thy judgments,
    For thou hast established law for me.
103 How sweet to my taste are thy teachings,
    Sweeter than honey in my mouth.

---

* This translates the Greek word *mese* and denotes the point where, during the Orthodox Matins for the departed, Psalm 118 is divided in half, as opposed to the usual division into three stases.

104 From thy commandments I won comprehension,
   Therefore I hated every false way.

NUN

105 Thy word is a lamp to my feet
   And a light to my paths.
106 I swore an oath and confirmed it,
   To keep the judgments of thy righteousness.
107 I have been deeply humbled, O Lord,
   Quicken me according to thy word.
108 Receive, O Lord, my mouth's free tribute,
   And teach me thy judgments.
109 My soul is always in thy hands,
   I have never forgotten thy law.
110 The wicked have set snares for me,
   But I never strayed from thy commandments.
111 I have inherited thy testimonies forever,
   They are my heart's rejoicing.
112 I set my heart to do thy statutes
   Forever, as a recompense.

SAMEK

113 Transgressors I have hated,
   But I have loved thy law.
114 Thou art my helper and protector,
   I have placed my hope in thy word.
115 Depart from me, you evildoers,
   I shall search deeply my God's commandments.
116 Uphold me according to thy teaching,
   And I shall live,
   Do not disgrace my expectation.
117 Sustain me and I shall be saved,
   I shall meditate always in thy statutes.
118 Thou despisest all who spurn thy statutes,
   For their inward thought is wicked.
119 I counted as transgressors all of earth's sinners,
   I have always loved thy testimonies.
120 Pierce my flesh with fear of thee,

For I have feared thy judgments.

AYIN

121 I have done judgment and righteousness,
Do not deliver me to my tormentors.
122 Vouch for thy servant's goodness,
Let not the arrogant falsely accuse me.
123 My eyes dimmed in awaiting thy salvation,
The teaching of thy righteousness.
124 Deal with thy servant in thy mercy,
And teach me thy statutes.
125 I am thy servant, make me comprehend,
And I shall know thy testimonies.
126 It is time for the Lord to act,
They have shattered thy law.
127 I have therefore loved thy commandments
More than gold and precious stone.
128 Therefore I have been guided rightly
Into keeping all thy commandments,
And I have hated every false way.

PE

129 Wondrous are thy testimonies,
My soul therefore deeply searched them.
130 The revelation of thy words illumines,
And even infants comprehend.
131 I opened my mouth, I drew in my breath,
I longed for thy commandments.

Glory. Both now. Alleluia.

Look upon me and have mercy on me,
According to the judgment
Of those who love thy name.
133 Direct my steps by thy teaching,
And let no iniquity rule over me.

134 Set me free from every man's slander
   And I will keep thy commandments.
135 Make thy countenance shine upon thy servant
   And teach me thy statutes.
136 My eyes have poured streams of tears
   Because men have not kept thy law.

TSADDE

137 Righteous art thou, O Lord,
   And upright is thy judgment.
138 The testimonies thou hast commanded
   Are vast righteousness and truth.
139 The zeal of thy house has consumed me,
   For my enemies have forgotten thy words.
140 Thy teaching is purified in fire,
   Thy servant has deeply loved it.
141 I am small and counted as nothing,
   But I have never forgotten thy statutes.
142 Thy righteousness is everlasting righteousness
   And thy law is the truth.
143 Affliction and anguish have found me,
   But thy commandments are my meditation.
144 Thy testimonies are forever righteousness,
   Give me comprehension, and I shall live.

QOPH

145 I cried with my whole heart:
   Hear me, O Lord,
   I shall search deeply thy statutes.
146 I cried out to thee: Save me,
   I shall keep thy testimonies.
147 I have arisen in the night's depths,
   Crying: In thy words I have hoped.
148 My eyes awoke before the dawn
   To meditate in thy teachings.
149 Hear my voice, O Lord, in thy mercy,
   Quicken me in thy judgment.
150 Those wrongly hounding me draw near,

Having drawn far from thy law.
151 How very near thou art, O Lord,
All thy commandments are truth,
152 And long have I known from thy testimonies
That thou hast founded them forever.

RESH

153 Behold my humiliation and rescue me,
For I have never forgotten thy law.
154 Plead my cause and redeem me,
Quicken me according to thy word.
155 Salvation is far from all sinners,
They never searched deeply thy statutes.
156 Many are thy compassions, O Lord,
Quicken me according to thy judgment.
157 Many are those who pursue and afflict me,
But never have I swerved from thy testimonies.
158 I beheld those indifferent to God,
And I wasted away;
They have never kept thy teachings.
159 I have loved deeply thy commandments;
Quicken me, O Lord, in thy mercy.
160 The beginning of thy words is truth,
The judgments of thy righteousness
Endure for all ages.

SHIN

161 Princes have pursued me for no cause,
But my heart feared only thy words.
162 I shall rejoice in thy teachings
Like one finding great treasure.
163 Injustice I have hated and abhorred,
Thy law I have deeply loved.
164 Seven times a day I have praised thee
For the judgments of thy righteousness.
165 Great peace have all those
Who keep on loving thy law;
There is no stumbling block for them.

166 I have longed for thy salvation, O Lord,
   I have deeply loved thy commandments.
167 My soul has kept thy testimonies,
   I have loved them very deeply.
168 I kept thy commandments and testimonies,
   For all my ways are before thee.

TAU

169 Let my cry come near thee, O Lord:
   Make me comprehend fully thy teaching.
170 Let my petition come before thee:
   According to thy teaching, rescue me.
171 My lips shall overflow in song
   When thou teachest me thy statutes.
172 My tongue shall speak of thy teaching,
   For all thy commandments are righteousness.
173 Let thy hand be there to save me,
   For I have chosen thy commandments.
174 O Lord, I have longed for thy salvation
   And thy law is my meditation.
175 My soul shall live and praise thee,
   And thy judgments shall help me.
176 I have gone astray like a lost sheep,
   Seek out thy servant,
   I have never forgotten thy commandments.

          Glory. Both now. Alleluia.

KATHISMA EIGHTEEN

PSALM 119
An ode of the Ascents.

IN MY AFFLICTION I CRIED out to the Lord, and he heard me:
2 Rescue my soul, O Lord, from unjust lips, from a treacherous tongue.
3 What must be given to thee, what must be added to thee against this treacherous tongue?
4 The warrior's arrows sharpened with hot coals from the desert.
5 Ah my God! My exile never ends, so long have I dwelt in the tents of Kedar,

6 So long has my soul been exiled.
7 I kept on being peaceful with those hating peace, when I spoke with them they kept on hating me for no cause.

PSALM 120
An ode of the Ascents.

I LIFTED MY EYES to the mountains: From whence shall my help come?
2 My help comes from the Lord who fashioned heaven and earth.
3 May thy foot never misstep, may thy guardian never slumber.
4 Behold: the guardian of Israel shall never slumber nor sleep.
5 The Lord shall keep guard over thee, the Lord is thy shelter at thy right hand.
6 All day the sun shall not harm thee nor shall the moon in the night.
7 The Lord shall guard thee from all evil, the Lord shall guard thy very soul,
8 The Lord shall guard thy coming and going from henceforth and forevermore.

PSALM 121
An ode of the Ascents.

I WAS DELIGHTED in those who had said to me: We shall go to the Lord's house.
2 Our feet have stood within thy courts, O Jerusalem.
3 Jerusalem is being built as a city where all dwell in concord,
4 Where the tribes have gone up, the tribes of the Lord, in testimony to Israel, to give thanks to the name of the Lord.
5 There the thrones of judgment were set, thrones over the house of David.
6 Pray now for the peace of Jerusalem, for abundance to those who love thee.
7 May peace be now in thy might, abundance in thy strong towers.
8 For my brothers' and companions' sake I have asked peace for thee.
9 For the sake of our Lord's house I have deeply sought out good things for thee.

PSALM 122
An Ode of the Ascents.

I HAVE LIFTED MY eyes up to thee, O thou who dwellest in the heavens.
2 Behold: as servants' eyes look to the hands of their masters, as the eyes of the maidservant to her mistress' hands, so our eyes look to our Lord God until he have mercy on us.
3 Have mercy on us, O Lord, have mercy on us, for we have had greatly more than our fill of contempt,
4 Our soul has been greatly filled: A disgrace to the wealthy, the contempt of the proud.

PSALM 123
An ode of the Ascents.

HAD NOT THE LORD been among us—let Israel now say—
2 Had not the Lord been among us when men rose up against us,
3 They would have swallowed us whole when their wrath raged against us,
4 The waters would have drowned us, our soul plunged into the torrent,
5 Our soul plunged all the way down into the overwhelming waters.
6 Blessed be the Lord, who has not abandoned us as prey to their teeth.
7 Our soul has escaped like a sparrow from a hunter's snare, the snare has been shattered and we have escaped.
8 Our help is in the name of the Lord, who made heaven and earth.

Glory. Both now. Alleluia.

PSALM 124
An ode of the Ascents.

THOSE WHO TRUST in the Lord are like Mount Zion; he who dwells in Jerusalem shall be forever unshaken.
2 The mountains surround her and the Lord surrounds his people henceforth and forevermore.

3 The Lord will never permit the scepter of wickedness to rule the land of the righteous, lest the righteous reach out to work evil with their own hands.
4 Do good, O Lord, to the good, to the upright in heart.
5 But those who go straying into intricate tangles, the Lord shall lead them away with the workers of wickedness. Peace be upon Israel.

PSALM 125
An ode of the Ascents.

WHEN THE LORD had brought back the captives of Zion, we became like those who are given great comfort.
2 Then our mouth filled with joy, our tongue with exultation, then even the nations shall say: The Lord did great things for them.
3 The Lord did great things for us, we have become filled with gladness.
4 Bring back, O Lord, our captives, like torrents rushing in the dry south.
5 Those who sow with tears shall reap with rejoicing.
6 Those who went forth in tears bearing their seed with them shall return with rejoicing, bearing great fruit with them.

PSALM 126
An ode of the Ascents, for Solomon.

UNLESS THE LORD build the house, the builders have toiled in vain; unless the Lord watch the city, in vain has the watchman kept awake.
2 In vain do you rise at daybreak rousing yourselves from your rest to eat the bread of sorrows, since he gave his beloved ones sleep.
3 Behold, sons are the Lord's inheritance, the fruit of the womb his reward.
4 Like arrows in a warrior's hand, so are the sons of the released.
5 Blessed is the man who shall see his desires for his sons fulfilled; they shall never be ashamed to speak with their enemies at the gate.

PSALM 127
An ode of the Ascents.

BLESSED ARE ALL those fearing the Lord, all those who walk in his ways.
2. Thou shalt eat the fruits of thy labor, thou art blessed, it shall go well for thee.
3. Thy wife shall be like a vine flourishing on all sides of thy house, thy sons like olive shoots all around thy table.
4. Behold, thus shall be blessed the man fearing the Lord.
5. May the Lord bless thee from Zion, mayest thou see the good of Jerusalem all the days of thy life,
6. Mayest thou see the sons of thy sons. Peace be upon Israel.

PSALM 128
An ode of the Ascents.

SINCE MY YOUTH they have often attacked me—let Israel now say—
2. Since my youth they have often attacked me, yet they have never prevailed over me.
3. Behind my back, the sinners kept scheming, they kept increasing their wickedness.
4. But the righteous Lord has cut asunder the necks of the sinners.
5. Let all those who hate Zion be disgraced and turned back.
6. Let them be like grass on the housetops that withers before it can grow,
7. Grass with which the reaper has never filled his hand, grass with which no sheaf-gatherer has ever filled his arms,
8. And let no passerby say to them: The Lord's blessing be with you, in the Lord's name we have blessed you.

Glory. Both now. Alleluia.

PSALM 129
An ode of the Ascents.

From out of the depths, O Lord, I have cried out to thee,
2 O Lord, hear my voice, let thine ears be attentive to the voice of my supplications.
3 If thou, Lord, shouldst mark iniquities, O Lord, who could stand?
4 For with thee is forgiveness.
5 For thy name's sake, O Lord, I have patiently waited for thee, my soul went on patiently waiting for thy word, my soul has hoped in the Lord.
6 From the morning watch until night, from the morning watch let Israel hope in the Lord.
7 For with the Lord there is mercy, with him is abundant redemption,
8 And he shall redeem Israel from out of all his iniquities.

PSALM 130
An ode of the Ascents, for David.

My heart, O Lord, has not been exalted, I have not raised up my eyes, nor have I wandered about in things too great or too marvelous for me.
2 For if I had not kept my mind forever in humility, but had exalted my soul like a child weaned from his mother, so thou wouldst requite my soul.
3 Let Israel hope in the Lord from henceforth and forevermore.

PSALM 131
An ode of the Ascents.

Remember David, O Lord, and all his humility,
2 How he vowed to the Lord, swearing this oath to Jacob's God:
3 I shall not enter into the house where I dwell, I shall not lie down upon the bed where I rest,
4 I shall not give my eyes any sleep, nor give my eyelids any slumber, nor give any rest to my temples
5 Until I find a place for the Lord, a tabernacle for Jacob's God.
6 Behold, we heard of it in Ephrathah, we found it in forest clearings.

7 Let us enter into his tabernacle, let us worship where his feet have stood.
8 Arise, O Lord, go up into thy rest, thou and the ark of thy sanctity.
9 Thy priests shall vest in righteousness, thy saints shall shout for joy.
10 For thy servant David's sake, do not turn away from the face of thy Christ.
11 The Lord swore to David this truth and he shall never retract it: I shall set upon thy throne the fruit of thine own flesh.
12 If thy sons shall keep my covenant and the testimonies I shall teach them, then their sons shall sit forevermore upon thy throne.
13 For the Lord has chosen Zion, he has chosen her for his dwelling:
14 This is forever my place of rest, here I shall always dwell, for I have chosen her.
15 I shall bless her hunts with blessings, I shall satisfy her poor with bread.
16 With salvation I shall clothe her priests, her saints shall exult with joy.
17 There I shall make spring up a horn for David, and I shall ready a lamp for my Christ.
18 His enemies I shall clothe in shame, upon him shall my sanctification flourish.

PSALM 132
An ode of the Ascents, for David.

Behold the beauty and delight when brothers dwell in unity. 2 It is like oil of myrrh upon the head running down on the beard, running down the beard of Aaron, running to his garment's lowest hem.
3 It is like the dew of Hermon running down the mountains of Zion, for there the Lord commanded blessing and life forevermore.

PSALM 133
An ode of the Ascents.

Behold, bless the Lord, all you servants of the Lord, you who stand in the Lord's house, in the courts of the house of our God.

Kathisma Eighteen

2 In the nights, raise up your hands to his holy places and bless the Lord.
3 May the Lord bless you from Zion, he who made heaven and earth.

Glory. Both now. Alleluia.

KATHISMA NINETEEN

PSALM 134
Alleluia.

PRAISE THE NAME of the Lord, O you servants, praise the Lord,
2 You who stand in the Lord's house, in the courts of the house of our God.
3 Praise the Lord, for the Lord is good, sing praises to his name for it is beautiful,
4 For the Lord chose Jacob for himself, Israel for his special treasure.
5 For I know that the Lord is great, our Lord is above all other gods.
6 All the Lord willed, he has done, in heaven and on the earth, in the seas and in all deep places.

7   Raising clouds from earth's ends, he made lightning for the rains, bringing winds from his storehouses.
8   He struck down the firstborn of Egypt, both of man and of beast.
9   He sent forth signs and portents into thy midst, O Egypt, among Pharaoh and all his servants.
10 He struck down many nations, and he destroyed mighty kings,
11 Sihon king of the Amorites, and Og king of Bashan, and all the kingdoms of Canaan,
12 And he gave their lands as inheritance, an inheritance for Israel his people.
13 Thy name, O Lord, endures forever, thy memorial, O Lord, for all generations.
14 For the Lord will judge his people, he will give comfort to his servants.
15 The idols of nations are silver and gold, the works of men's hands.
16 They have mouths, but shall never speak, eyes they have, but shall never see,
17 They have ears, but shall never hear, nor is there any breath in their mouths.
18 May their makers become like them, and all who put their trust in them.
19 Bless the Lord, O house of Israel, bless the Lord, O house of Aaron,
20 Bless the Lord, O Levi's house, you that fear the Lord, bless the Lord!
21 Blessed be the Lord out of Zion, he who dwells in Jerusalem.

PSALM 135
Alleluia.

GIVE THANKS TO the Lord, for he is good, for his mercy endures forever.
2   Give thanks to the God of gods, for his mercy endures forever.
3   Give thanks to the Lord of lords, for his mercy endures forever.
4   To him who alone does great wonders, for his mercy endures forever.
5   Who has made the heavens in wisdom, for his mercy endures forever.

6 Who made firm the earth on the waters, for his mercy endures forever.
7 Who alone made the great lights, for his mercy endures forever.
8 The sun to rule over the day, for his mercy endures forever.
9 The moon and stars to rule the night, for his mercy endures forever.
10 Who struck down Egypt and their firstborn, for his mercy endures forever.
11 Who led Israel out from their midst, for his mercy endures forever.
12 With mighty hand and upraised arm, for his mercy endures forever.
13 Who divided the Red Sea in two, for his mercy endures forever.
14 And led Israel out from amidst it, for his mercy endures forever.
15 And who overthrew Pharaoh and all his host in the Red Sea, for his mercy endures forever.
16 Who led his people through the wilderness, for his mercy endures forever; who drew water from the split rock, for his mercy endures forever.
17 Who struck down mighty kings, for his mercy endures forever.
18 And destroyed powerful kings, for his mercy endures forever.
19 Sihon king of the Amorites, for his mercy endures forever.
20 And Og king of Bashan, for his mercy endures forever.
21 Who gave their land as inheritance, for his mercy endures forever.
22 An inheritance for Israel his servant, for his mercy endures forever.
23 For in our humbled and lowly state, the Lord always remembered us, for his mercy endures forever.
24 And he redeemed us from our enemies, for his mercy endures forever.
25 Who provides food for all creatures, for his mercy endures forever.
26 O give thanks to the God of heaven, for his mercy endures forever.

PSALM 136

A psalm of David, concerning Jeremiah in the captivity.

BY THE RIVERS of Babylon, there we sat down and wept when we remembered Zion.
2 Upon the willows in her midst, we hung up our harps.

3 There, our captors asked us for some words from our songs, our plunderers demanded and said: Sing us a psalm of Zion.
4 How shall we sing the Lord's song in a strange and alien land?
5 If I forget thee, O Jerusalem, let my right hand wither,
6 Let my tongue cleave to my mouth if I do not remember thee, if I do not keep Jerusalem as the fountainhead of my joy.
7 Remember, O Lord, Edom's sons on that day in Jerusalem, saying: Destroy it, destroy it, down to the very foundations.
8 O wretched daughter of Babylon, blessed the one who shall deal to thee what thou hast dealt to us,
9 Blessed the one who shall seize thine infants and smash them against the rock.

Glory. Both now. Alleluia.

PSALM 137
A psalm of David, concerning Haggai and Zacharias.

I SHALL PRAISE THEE, O Lord, with my whole heart, and because thou hast heard all the words of my mouth, I shall sing psalms to thee in the very presence of angels.
2 I shall fall down in worship toward thy holy temple, and I shall sing to thy name for thy mercy and thy truth, for thou hast magnified thy teaching above even thy name.
3 On the day I shall call out to thee, hear me speedily, for thou shalt care greatly for my soul in thy strength.
4 O Lord, let all of earth's kings sing their praise to thee, for they have heard all the words of thy mouth,
5 Let them sing in the Lord's ways, for immense is the Lord's glory.
6 Though the Lord is exalted, he keeps watch over the humble, but the proud he knows from afar.
7 If I walk amidst agonies thou shalt make me live, for against my enemies' wrath thou hast stretched forth thy hand; thy right hand has saved me.
8 Thou shalt repay them, O Lord, for me; thy mercy, O Lord, endures forever, never despise the works of thy hands.

PSALM 138
For the end of the struggle, a psalm of David concerning Zacharias in the diaspora.

THOU HAST TESTED me greatly, O Lord, thou hast known me.
2 Thou hast known when I sat or I stood, discerning my thoughts from afar,
3 Exploring my path and my travels, and thou hast foreseen all my ways,
4 For deceit is never on my tongue.
5 Behold, O Lord, thou hast known all things, last things and first; thou hast fashioned me, placing thy hands upon me.
6 Such knowledge has been wondrous for me, so strong I cannot fully grasp it.
7 Where could I go from thy Spirit? Where flee from thy countenance?
8 If I rise up to heaven, thou art there, if I go down to Hades, thou art there.
9 Were I to spread out my wings and fly straight to the dawn, taking up home in the sea's farthest reach,
10 Even there shall thy hand lead me, thy right hand shall hold fast to me.
11 I thought darkness would surely kill me, but to my delight even the night shall shine,
12 For darkness shall never be dark with thee, the night shall be bright as day, darkness and light one and the same.
13 For thou hast possessed my deepest heart, O Lord, thou hast taken hold of me even from my mother's womb.
14 I shall give praise to thee, O Lord, for I am fearfully and wondrously made; marvelous are thy works, very deeply my soul knows this.
15 My frame thou didst invisibly fashion was never hidden from thee, nor was my substance ever hidden in the earth's lowest depths.
16 Thine eyes beheld me yet unformed; all men shall be written in thy book, they shall be fashioned continually when there are yet none of them.
17 Thy beloved friends, O God, have become greatly precious to me, their authority become greatly strong.

18 I shall count them and they shall increase more than the sands of the sea; I awake and I am still with thee.
19 If only, O God, thou wouldst slay sinners; O violent men of blood, depart from me.
20 For thou wilt say about their thoughts: Vainly shall they seize thy cities.
21 Have I not hated, Lord, those hating thee? Have I not kept wasting away because of thine enemies?
22 I hated them with perfect hatred, I counted them my enemies.
23 Test me greatly, O God, know my heart, examine me and know all my paths,
24 See if any wicked way be within me, and lead me in the way everlasting.

PSALM 139
For the end of the struggle, a psalm of David.

Deliver me, O Lord, from the evil man; rescue me from the violent ones
2 Who have devised evil in their hearts, provoking conflicts all the day long.
3 They have sharpened their serpent tongues, snake's venom is under their lips.   *Selah*
4 Protect me, O Lord, from the sinner's hand, free me from those violent men who schemed to overthrow my goings.
5 The arrogant have laid a snare for me, a net of snares spread for my feet, a stumbling block on my path for me.   *Selah*
6 I said to the Lord: Thou art my God; hear, O Lord, the sound of my prayer.
7 O Lord, Lord, might of my salvation, thou hast shielded my head on the day of war.
8 Never, O Lord, hand me over to the strong desires of the wicked, for they have schemed against me; never abandon me, lest they triumph.   *Selah*
9 Let the work of their own lips cover even the chief of those who surround me.
10 Let fiery coals fall upon them, let them go down into the flames, let the agony be unbearable.

11 Never let a slanderer flourish on earth, let evils hound a wicked man to destruction.
12 I know that the Lord will uphold the cause of the afflicted, he shall give justice for the poor.
13 Surely the righteous shall sing praise to thy name, surely the upright shall dwell in thy presence.

Glory. Both now. Alleluia.

PSALM 140
A psalm of David.

O Lord, I called upon thee, hear me, receive the voice of my prayer when I call upon thee.
2 Let my prayer arise in thy sight as incense, let the lifting up of my hands be an evening sacrifice.
3 Set a guard, O Lord, over my mouth, a strong door about my lips.
4 Incline not my heart to evil words that ease the way for evil men to work their wicked deeds; let me not join their inner circles.
5 The righteous man shall chastise me with sweet mercy, and correct me, but the sweet oil of sinners shall never touch my head, for my prayer shall continually be against their delights.
6 Their judges were smashed on the rock, although they had heard my words, heard how sweet they were.
7 Their bones were all scattered in Hades, like an earth-clod broken on the earth.
8 For my eyes, O Lord, Lord, look to thee, in thee have I hoped, let not my soul slip away.
9 Preserve me from the snares they have spread out for me, from the stumbling block set out for me by the workers of wickedness.
10 Let the wicked fall into their own nets, all of them together, while I alone pass through.

PSALM 141
Instruction by David, when he was in the cave, praying.

WITH MY VOICE I cried out to the Lord, with my voice I prayed to the Lord.
2 Before him I shall pour out my prayer, in his presence declare my afflictions.
3 When my spirit fainted within me, then thou knewest my paths, for on the way I was going they had hidden a snare for me.
4 I looked on my right, and I saw that no one had recognized me, that all flight had failed me, that no one saw deeply my soul.
5 I cried out to thee, O Lord, saying: Thou art my hope, my share in the land of the living.
6 Attend unto my prayer for I am brought very low, free me from my tormentors for they are stronger than I.
7 Bring my soul out of prison, O Lord, that I may sing praise to thy name; the righteous shall patiently wait until thou shalt deal richly with me.

PSALM 142
A psalm of David, when his son Absalom pursued him.

O LORD, HEAR MY PRAYER; in thy truthfulness heed my plea, answer me in thy righteousness.
2 Do not judge against thy servant, for no man living shall be found to be righteous in thy sight.
3 For the enemy has tormented my soul, he has laid low my life to the earth, making me dwell in dark places like one who has been long dead,
4 And my spirit has fallen into depression, my heart deeply troubled within me.
5 I remembered the days of old, I meditated on all thy works, and deeply on the creations of thy hands.
6 I spread out my hands to thee, my soul thirsts like dry land for thee.   *Selah*
7 Hear me speedily, O Lord, my spirit has forsaken me; turn not thy face from me or I shall become like one who goes down into the pit.

8 Grant that I may hear every morning thy mercy, for in thee I have hoped; and grant me, O Lord, to know the way wherein I should walk, for I have lifted my soul up to thee.
9 Deliver me, O Lord, from my enemies, for to thee I have fled.
10 Teach me to do thy will, for thou art my God, thy good Spirit shall guide me into the land of uprightness.
11 For thy name's sake, O Lord, thou shalt quicken me to life, in thy righteousness thou shalt bring my soul out from these afflictions.
12 In thy mercy thou shalt destroy my enemies, thou shalt completely unmake all those tormenting my soul, for I am thy servant.

Glory. Both now. Alleluia.

KATHISMA TWENTY

PSALM 143
David's, concerning Goliath.

BLESSED IS THE LORD my God, who trains my hands for battle, my fingers to make war.

2 He is my mercy and my refuge, my helper and my savior, my protector in whom I have hoped, who subdues my people under me.

3 Lord, what is man that thou hast revealed thyself to him, or the son of man that thou hast bent thy thought to him?

4 Man has become an empty thing, his days passing like shadows.

5 O Lord, bend thy heavens and descend, touch the mountains, they shall smoke,

6 Send lightning, thou shalt scatter them, shoot thine arrows, thou shalt panic them.

7 Reach down thy hand from on high, free me and save me from great waters, from the hands of strange men
8 Whose mouth has spoken empty things, whose right hand has dealt violence.
9 I shall sing a new song, O Lord, to thee, I shall play to thee on a harp of ten strings—
10 To the One who gives salvation to kings, who redeems David his servant from an evil man's sword.
11 Free me and save me from strange hands, from the mouths that speak emptiness, from right hands that deal violence.
12 Their sons are like freshly ripened shoots, their daughters like glorious palaces.
13 Their storehouses are all filled, bursting with abundance on all sides, their flocks multiply as they go.
14 Their oxen are grown immense, there is no break in their fences, nor any shouting in their squares.
15 Happy the people whose lot this is, but blessed are those people whose God is the Lord.

PSALM 144
David's, a psalm of praise.

I SHALL EXALT THEE, my God and my King, I shall bless thy name forever and unto ages of ages.
2 Every day I shall bless thee and sing praises to thy name forever and unto ages of ages.
3 Great is the Lord and greatly to be praised; his greatness exceeds every measure.
4 All generations shall praise thy works, they shall declare thy mighty power,
5 They shall speak of the great glory that is the majesty of thy holiness, they shall recount thy wondrous works.
6 They shall speak of the power of thy fearsome deeds, they shall recount thy great majesty.
7 From them shall pour forth the memory of thy rich goodness, they shall rejoice in thy righteousness.
8 The Lord is gracious and merciful, longsuffering and abundant in mercy.
9 The Lord is gracious to all, his mercies are on all his works.

10 Lord, let all thy works praise thee, and let all thy saints bless thee.
11 They shall tell of thy kingdom's glory and they shall speak of thy lordship,
12 So all the sons of men may know thy lordship and the glory of thy kingdom's magnificence.
13 Thy kingdom is a kingdom for all ages, thy dominion is unto ages of ages.
14 The Lord is faithful in his words and he is holy in all his works.
15 The Lord steadies all those who stumble, he lifts up all those struck down.
16 All eyes look to thee in hope, thou givest them their food in due season.
17 Thou openest thy hand and all living things are satisfied in thy good pleasure.
18 The Lord is righteous in all his ways and he is holy in all his works.
19 The Lord is near to all who call on him, to all who call upon him in truth.
20 He shall do the will of those fearing him, he shall hear their supplications, and he shall save them.
21 The Lord preserves all who love him, but all sinners he shall utterly destroy.
22 My mouth shall speak the Lord's praise; let all flesh bless his holy name from henceforth and forevermore.

Glory. Both now. Alleluia.

PSALM 145
Alleluia, concerning Haggai and Zacharias.

Praise the Lord, O my soul.
2 I shall praise the Lord in my life, I shall sing to my God my whole life.
3 Put not your trust in princes in whom there is no salvation.
4 His breath shall depart, he shall return to the earth; on that day all his thoughts shall crumble.
5 Blessed is the one whose help is in the God of Jacob, whose hope is in the Lord his God,
6 In him who made heaven and earth, the sea and everything in them, who preserves forever the truth,

7 Who provides justice for the wronged, who provides food for the starving. The Lord sets every prisoner free,
8 The Lord uplifts the afflicted, the Lord gives wisdom to the blind, the Lord loves greatly the righteous.
9 The Lord keeps watch over strangers, he shall adopt the orphan and widow, but he shall unmake every sinner's way.
10 The Lord shall forever be King, thy God, O Zion, to all generations.

PSALM 146
Alleluia, concerning Haggai and Zacharias.

PRAISE THE LORD, for to sing psalms is good, let praise be sweet to our God.
2 In rebuilding Jerusalem, the Lord shall regather all Israel's outcasts,
3 He shall heal the shattered in heart, he shall bind up all their wounds.
4 He measures the multitude of stars, calling each of them by its name.
5 Great is our Lord, great is his power, his understanding exceeds every measure.
6 The Lord raises up the meek but casts down the wicked to earth.
7 Strike up a paean of praise to the Lord, sing praise to our God with the harp,
8 Who covers the heavens with clouds, who readies the rains for the earth, who makes grass grow on the mountains and the vegetation that men consume.
9 He gives fodder to their cattle, and food to the raven's brood when they call out to him.
10 Never shall he prize the horse's strength nor value the swift legs of a man.
11 The Lord delights in those who fear him, in those who hope in his mercy.

PSALM 147
Alleluia, concerning Haggai and Zacharias.

SING PRAISE to the Lord, O Jerusalem; praise thy God, O Zion,
2 For he has made strong thy gates, he has blessed thy sons within thee,

3 Who grants peace to thy borders, filling thee with the finest of wheat.
4 He sends his teaching to earth where his word shall run very swiftly.
5 When he gives snow thick as wool, sprinkling the mists like ashes,
6 Casting forth hailstones like crumbs, who shall withstand his icy cold?
7 He shall send his word and melt them, he shall breathe out his breath and the waters shall flow,
8 Declaring his word unto Jacob, his statutes and judgments to Israel.
9 Never did he so with other nations, never has he shown his judgments to them.

Glory. Both now. Alleluia.

PSALM 148
Alleluia, concerning Haggai and Zacharias.

Praise the Lord from the heavens, praise him in the highest,
2 Praise him, all you his angels, praise him, all you his hosts,
3 Praise him, sun and moon, praise him, all you shining stars,
4 Praise him, you heavens of heavens, and you waters above the heavens.
5 Let them praise the Lord's name, for he spoke and they came to be, he commanded and they were created.
6 He has established them forever and unto ages of ages; he has set forth his ordinance and it shall never pass away.
7 Praise the Lord from under the earth, you serpents and all the deeps,
8 Fire and hail, snow and ice, stormy wind fulfilling his word,
9 Mountains and all the hills, fruitful trees and all cedars,
10 Wild beasts and all cattle, creeping things and wild birds,
11 Kings of the earth and all peoples, princes and all judges of the earth,
12 Both young men and maidens, elders together with children:
13 Let them praise the Lord's name, for his name alone is exalted, his splendor is over earth and heaven.

14   He shall exalt the horn of his people, a hymn to his holy people, to the sons of Israel, to all people who draw near unto him.

PSALM 149
Alleluia.

Sing to the Lord a new song, his praise in the church of his saints.
2   Let Israel rejoice in his Maker, let Zion's sons exult in their King.
3   Let them praise his name with the dance; with tambourine and harp let them sing psalms to him.
4   For the Lord delights in his people, he shall exalt the meek in salvation.
5   The saints shall rejoice in glory, let them exult on their beds,
6   The high praise of God in their mouth, a two-edged sword in their hand,
7   To deal retribution to the nations, chastisement to all the peoples,
8   To shackle their kings with chains, their nobles with fetters of iron,
9   To accomplish the doom decreed against them: This glory shall all his saints have.

PSALM 150
Alleluia.

Praise God for his saints, praise him for his steady strength,
2   Praise him for his mighty acts, praise him according to the full abundance of his greatness.
3   Praise him with the trumpet's blare, praise him with the harp and lyre,
4   Praise him with tambourine and dance, praise him with strings and flutes,
5   Praise him with resounding cymbals, praise him with triumphant cymbals,
6   Let every breath praise the Lord.

Glory. Both now. Alleluia.

ІС · ХС НІ · КА

BIBLIOGRAPHY

Alter, Robert. *The Art of Biblical Narrative*. New York: Basic Books, 1981.

Breck, John. *The Shape of Biblical Language*. Crestwood, NY: St. Vladimir Seminary Press, 1994.

Brenton, Lancelot C. L. *The Interlineary Hebrew and English Psalter*. Grand Rapids, MI: Zondervan, 1979.

———. *The Septuagint Version, Greek and English*. Grand Rapids, MI: Zondervan, 1970.

Brown, Francis, et al. *The New Brown-Driver-Briggs-Gesenius Hebrew and English Lexicon*. Peabody, MA: Hendrickson, 1979.

Cassiodorus. *Explanation of the Psalms*. Vol. 1. Mahwah, NJ: Paulist Press, 1990.

Florovsky, G., to S. Sakharov. May 15, 1958. In: Arkhimandrit Sofronii [Sakharov], *Perepiska s Protoiereem Georgiem Florovskim*. Essex/Moscow: Svyato-Ioanno-Predtechenskii Monastyr'/Svyato-Troitskaya Sergieva Lavra, 2008.

George, Archimandrite. *Theosis: The True Purpose of Human Life*. Mount Athos, Greece: Holy Monastery of St. Gregorios, 2006. Also available online at http://orthodoxinfo.com/general/theosis-english.pdf.

Hatch, Edwin, and Henry A. Redpath. *A Concordance to the Septuagint*. 2nd edition. Grand Rapids, MI: Baker Books, 1998.

Heine, Ronald F. *Gregory of Nyssa's Treatise on the Inscriptions of the Psalms*. New York: Oxford University Press, 1995.

St. Isaac the Syrian. *Ascetical Homilies*. Brookline, MA: Holy Transfiguration Monastery, 1984. This book has now been corrected and reprinted and is available in a revised second edition.

Lampe, G. W. H. *A Patristic Greek Lexicon*. Oxford, UK: Clarendon Press, 1961.

Liddell, Henry G., and Robert Scott, with H. S. Jones and R. McKenzie. *A Greek-English Lexicon*. Oxford, UK: Clarendon Press, 1968.

Lossky, Vladimir. *In the Image and Likeness*. Crestwood, NY: SVS Press, 1974.

Bibliography

Lust, J., et al. *A Greek-English Lexicon of the Septuagint*. Stuttgart, Germany: Deutsche Bibelgessellschaft, 1992 (Part 1) and 1996 (Part 2).

Maria, Mother. *The Psalms: An Exploratory Translation*. North Yorkshire, UK: Greek Orthodox Monastery of the Assumption, 1973.

Peterson, Eugene H. *Leap Over a Wall*. New York: Harper, 1998.

Rahlfs, Alfred. *Septuaginta*. Stuttgart, Germany: Deutsche Bibelgessellschaft, 1979.

Taylor, Bernard A. *The Analytical Lexicon to the Septuagint*. Grand Rapids, MI: Zondervan, 1994.

Ware, Kallistos. "The Debate about Palamism." *Eastern Churches Review* IX: 1–2.

APPENDIX

Numbering of Psalms
and Praying the Kathismata

1. *Numbering of Psalms:*

SEPTUAGINT PSALM NUMBERS	HEBREW PSALM NUMBERS
1–8	1–8
9	9–10
10–112	11–113 (*add 1 to the number of each psalm*)
113	114–115
114	116:1–9
115	116:10–19
116–145	117–146 (*add 1 to the number of each psalm*)
146	147:1–11
147	147:12–20
148–150	148–150

Appendix

2. Order of Reading the Kathismata in Daily Prayer:*

DAY	MORNING	EVENING
Sunday	2, 3	*none*
Monday	4, 5	6
Tuesday	7, 8	9
Wednesday	10, 11	12
Thursday	13, 14	15
Friday	19, 20	18
Saturday	16, 17	1

3. Prayers after each stasis:

AFTER THE FIRST AND SECOND STASES OF EACH KATHISMA:

Glory to the Father and to the Son and to the Holy Spirit, both now and ever and unto ages of ages. Amen.

Alleluia. Alleluia. Alleluia. Glory to thee, O God. (*three times*)

Lord, have mercy. (*three times*)

Glory to the Father and to the Son and to the Holy Spirit, both now and ever and unto ages of ages. Amen.

AFTER THE FINAL STASIS OF EACH KATHISMA:

Glory to the Father and to the Son and to the Holy Spirit, both now and ever and unto ages of ages. Amen.

Alleluia. Alleluia. Alleluia. Glory to thee, O God. (*three times*)

---

* During Lent (the period of fasting in preparation for Pascha, or Easter), the Orthodox Church follows a different and intensified order of reading the Psalter. The rules for this and other variations can be found in the *Festal Menaion*: St. Tikhon's Seminary Press, 1998, pp. 533–534.